Dedication

This book is dedicated to the thousands of children in my life who give me inspiration and inner strength to do my part in creating a safe and caring world. It is my hope that these resources help connect children, parents, and educators so that they may achieve success wherever life takes them.

Acknowledgments

Safe & Caring Schools (SCS) has been tested where it matters most—in the classrooms. As such, my gratitude goes to all the teachers, specialists, and others who took time to incorporate the content of this guide into their lesson plans and then provide feedback about its efficacy. Efforts to create safe and caring schools are most effective when leadership is committed to applying the program at a schoolwide or district level to create systemic change. My thanks go to Dr. Wilfredo T. Laboy, superintendent of Lawrence Public Schools, and Dr. Mary Lou Bergeron, assistant superintendent of Lawrence Public Schools, for their foresight regarding the value of social and emotional learning in supporting students personally as well as academically. Dr. Bergeron has been particularly helpful in testing and proving this premise in schools.

Thanks to the staff at Free Spirit Publishing for their dedication to producing great products: To Publisher Judy Galbraith for her vision and belief in the power of the SCS program; John Kober, editor, for his ongoing support, guidance, patience and insight during the creation of the products, to Deb Anderson and Meg Bratsch, editors, for their extraordinary ability to produce resources that make a difference in the lives of students; and to the production team and all the others who pull the pieces together to make a book.

Thanks to J. Campbell at ArtVille for his professionalism, creativity, and ability to bring every page in this book to life. Also, thanks to my special educator friends, Kathy Kennedy Budge and Lynn Pauly, who listened, offered support, and used their ability to think outside the box to find the best way possible to connect with students.

This book series would not have been completed without the support of my wonderful family. My deepest gratitude goes to my husband, Steve Petersen, for the endless hours he worked by my side, for his ongoing encouragement, his incredible creativity, and for urging me to always reach for excellence. My heartfelt appreciation also goes to my daughter, Alexia, for her patience and support during this project and for reminding me daily about the true meaning of parenting. Warm thanks go to my parents for their unconditional love, for teaching me to believe in myself and encouraging me to follow my dreams.

> *"Safe & Caring Schools provides educators with the roadmap and all the tools necessary to transform classrooms and schools into environments that are not only physically, socially, and emotionally safe, but that engage and nurture our children's resilience, including their capacity and love for learning."*
>
> **BONNIE BENARD,**
> **SENIOR PROGRAM ASSOCIATE, WestEd,**
> **OAKLAND, CALIFORNIA**

CONTENTS

Part 1

Part 2

Part 3

SAFE & CARING SCHOOLS®

SKILLS FOR SCHOOL. SKILLS FOR LIFE.

GRADES 6–8

Katia S. Petersen, Ph.D.

free spirit
PUBLISHING®

Meeting kids'
social & emotional
needs since 1983

Library of Congress Cataloging-in-Publication Data
Petersen, Katia S.
  Safe & caring schools. Grades 6-8 : skills for school, skills for life / Katia S. Petersen.
    p. cm.
       ISBN-13: 978-1-57542-290-9
       ISBN-10: 1-57542-290-5
  1. Classroom management—United States. 2. School environment—United States. 3. Learning, Psychology of. I. Title. II. Title: Safe and caring schools. Grades 6-8.
       LB3013.P4336 2008
       372.1102—dc22

2008014671

Edited by Deborah Verdoorn Anderson and Meg Bratsch
Visual identity design by Tilka Design
Design by Tilka Design, and activity page design by J. Campbell, ArtVille
Illustrations by Brie Spangler

10 9 8 7 6 5 4 3 2 1
Printed in the United States of America

Free Spirit Publishing Inc.
217 Fifth Avenue North, Suite 200
Minneapolis, MN 55401-1299
(612) 338-2068
help4kids@freespirit.com
www.freespirit.com

FOREWORD

Dr. Katia Petersen has long been a champion for children and has dedicated her career to educating children and adults about the importance of social and emotional development in our youth and ourselves. Her vision, as a practitioner, has been to include life-skills education in the school day. She wants teachers to connect with students in a meaningful way and students to understand the relevance of school and how best to use it as a resource for self-development and well-being. Safe & Caring Schools is the culmination of more than 25 years of experience working in schools to help educators and others enhance the well-being and emotional literacy skills in children from preschool through high school.

In Safe & Caring Schools, Dr. Petersen has created a comprehensive approach to provide a solid foundation for infusing social and emotional literacy skills—including recognition of emotions, building relationships, conflict resolution, problem solving, decision making, and collaboration—into all areas of the program. The activities and resources provided in this book have been field-tested in classrooms across the United States with children from diverse backgrounds. Over the past years, I was fortunate enough to have worked with Dr. Petersen implementing Safe & Caring Schools in the Lawrence Public Schools. During the implementation, we collected a variety of data relative to overall school climate issues. In schools where Safe & Caring Schools was being implemented consistently, the data showed the following:

- an improvement in school climate
- greater parent engagement
- increased academic achievement
- a reduction in referrals for disciplinary infractions

We have continued to use the themes and activities of Safe & Caring Schools as a foundation for the social and emotional development of our students.

As an educator and school psychologist, I understand how children's levels of social and emotional literacy skill development impact their ability to succeed in school. I have seen firsthand how the development of these skills improved the overall academic and social success of our students. As an administrator, I am also acutely aware of the concerns that schools and school districts have relative to time on learning and adding new programs to the school day, especially at a time when there is a heightened focus on academic achievement and a demand for increased instructional time. With this in mind, Safe & Caring Schools was created to be an integrated component of systemic change at the classroom, school, and district levels. It has evolved into an easy-to-use, classroom-based approach that can be infused into all academic content areas with minimal effort on the part of teachers. The skills in the program are universal and can be addressed and reinforced throughout the school day and across grade levels. By infusing social and emotional learning across the curriculum, Safe & Caring Schools provides teachers with the flexibility and creativity they need to ensure students gain the skills they require to become successful students and members of society.

Mary Lou Bergeron, Ph.D.
Assistant Superintendent for
Operations and Support Services
Lawrence Public Schools
Lawrence, Massachusetts

PREFACE

Imagine a world where all children have an opportunity to learn and thrive—a safe place where adults help children become resilient. Imagine the impact safe and caring school communities can make in our challenging world as they encourage peer support, getting along, making ethical choices, problem solving, accountability, and cooperation. With this vision, I have created the Safe & Caring Schools (SCS) program to facilitate a blended curriculum of academic and social and emotional learning.

As times have changed, so have the demands put upon educators to meet the needs of every child. But one thing has never changed—the need for all children to feel appreciated, secure, and accepted. Many educators I speak to are concerned, and at times frustrated, about the lack of time to get everything done, the stress of how best to deal with challenging students, and the ever-growing issues of bullying and violence. Research increasingly supports that to reach the whole child, social and emotional learning (SEL) needs to be an integral part of the regular classroom curriculum. But, how much more can schools take on, what kind of support do they need, and how do they deal with the balancing act of mandated standards compliance and reaching children emotionally? SCS is a turnkey, literature-based program that supplies the school staff with a full suite of integrated materials to do this work, not as an add-on, but as part of the daily routine. Years of classroom testing have made Safe & Caring Schools a program that is easy to implement and sustain.

I've spent the past 27 years working in schools with staff and students of all ages, backgrounds, abilities, and talents. Using extensive feedback from thousands of educators, counselors, and parents, SCS addresses their needs by promoting social and emotional learning in the school, home, and community through the following:

- improving school climate and student behavior
- engaging and motivating students
- increasing academic achievement
- reducing stress
- increasing parent involvement
- enhancing staff teamwork

Time after time in testing this program, the schools that infused SEL into daily activities saw and felt a significant change in the behavior and language of their students. As attitudes and behaviors improved, so did academic performance. As teachers worked together making deliberate plans to embrace the SCS approach, they created systemic change in a natural way.

My hope is that the content and philosophy of this Safe & Caring Schools resource guide will inspire and help you to enhance your role as a significant adult in your students' lives. I have created a tool that helps you use your wisdom, energy, and desire to reach every child on a personal and emotional level. Every day is a new adventure and an opportunity to create a better world for our children. As you work with SCS materials, I welcome your feedback, success stories, and suggestions for improvements. You can write to me in care of:

Free Spirit Publishing
217 Fifth Avenue North, Suite 200
Minneapolis, MN 55401
or email me at help4kids@freespirit.com

Katia S. Petersen, Ph.D.

PART 1

Skills for School.
Skills for Life.

The mission of the Safe & Caring Schools (SCS) program is to create sustainable, positive systemic change by infusing social and emotional learning (SEL) and character education into daily academic instruction from preschool through grade 8. This takes place in partnership with educators, counselors, administrators, parents, and community members to improve academic achievement and school climate.

"When you educate the whole child, you can count on academic growth as well, even if that's not the primary intent." These words from "The Whole Child," a 2007 report from the Association for Supervision and Curriculum Development, reinforce the value of social and emotional learning. SEL is no longer seen as an option to be taught separately from academics; rather, it can be taught and implemented in schools in a number of ways.

SCS supports the idea that reaching the hearts of children is equally as important as reaching their minds. As one teacher who uses SCS explains, "I have learned that if I want my students to succeed academically, I need to teach them how to listen, follow directions, communicate effectively, resolve problems, and make good choices."

Teaching kids life skills needs to become part of the daily routine. Learning to get along with others, accepting responsibility for one's own actions, and making better choices takes practice and needs the guidance and ongoing support from the adults in kids' lives. Consistency and repetition, as well as modeling desirable behaviors, will increase students' ability to internalize and use new skills in real-life situations.

Research Foundation

For several years now, there has been a growing body of scientifically based research supporting the idea that enhanced social and emotional behaviors can have a strong impact on kids' success in school and, ultimately, in life (*Building Academic Success on Social and Emotional Learning: What Does the Research Say?* Edited by Joseph E. Zins, Roger P. Weissberg, Margaret C. Wang, and Herbert J. Walberg. Teachers College Press, Columbia University, 2004). The research substantiates that effective strategies for educational reform involve (1) a central focus on school climate change and (2) infusing SEL into regular academic lesson plans. Giving children a balance of intellectual and emotional instruction leads to more complete psychological development and helps them become better learners.

This idea is supported with hard data. For example, The Lucile Packard Foundation for Children's Health and the William T. Grant Foundation funded an analysis of 207 studies of social and emotional learning programs involving 288,000 elementary and secondary students from a cross section of urban, suburban, and rural schools. The results of the analysis are summarized in a 2008 report, "The Benefits of School-Based Social and Emotional Learning Programs" from CASEL (Collaborative for Academic, Social, and Emotional Learning). In evaluating academic outcomes, the study found that in schools where SEL is integrated into the regular programming, students scored 11 percentile points higher on standardized tests compared to students in schools not using an SEL program. Even though incorporating SEL activities required time in the school day, it did not negatively affect students' academic performance; rather, time spent on SEL improved academic performance. This project, conducted by Joseph A. Durlak of Loyola University in Chicago and Roger P. Weissberg at the University of Illinois at Chicago, was the first meta-analysis of research on the impact of SEL programs on students. Their full report is titled *The Effects of Social and Emotional Learning on the Behavior and Academic Performance of School Children*.

SCS incorporates a holistic approach in working with children, combining several research-based strategies into one program in order to nurture the whole child and promote student well being. SCS defines student well-being as "the development of knowledge, attitudes, skills, and behaviors that maximize students' functioning in environments where they live and work—school, home, and community" (Romano, J. L. *Journal of Educational Research,* 90, 1996). SCS provides you with a comprehensive set of core materials to enhance student well-being in a manner that is easily infused into your daily routine.

SCS materials incorporate a strengths-based approach that fosters resiliency in children to enable them to thrive and become successful in school and in life. Recent research shows that focusing on strengths is one of the key elements in supporting our youth, and schools play a critical role in the development of the strengths or assets in students.

- -

As Bonnie Benard writes in *Resiliency: What We Have Learned* (San Francisco: West Ed, 2004):

A framework, research support, and a rationale for resilience-based prevention and education include the following assumptions:

- Resilience is a capacity all youth have for healthy development and successful learning.
- Certain personal strengths are associated with healthy development and successful learning.
- Certain characteristics of families, schools, and communities are associated with the development of personal strengths and, in turn, healthy development and successful learning.
- Changing the life trajectories of children and youth from risk to resilience starts with changing the beliefs of the adults in their families, schools, and communities.

- -

SCS uses a complete and comprehensive plan that makes sense and works.

- It complements and enhances the well-being of children by promoting self-awareness, self-respect, integrity, and compassion to help them become productive citizens of any community.
- It encourages students to take risks and become active learners, regardless of their abilities, language barriers, or cultural differences.
- It leads students to make connections with the world around them by creating opportunities to practice the skills they need to face daily challenges.
- It allows students to reach for their full potential of becoming positive leaders by promoting social and emotional education as part of academic learning.

SCS activities support standards and comply with best practices for SEL infusion at school while providing opportunities for you, the teacher, to use your creativity. When aligned with the key competencies of the Collaborative for Academic, Social, and Emotional Learning (CASEL), the SCS activities clearly address those key SEL competencies: 1) Awareness of self and others, 2) Positive attitudes and values, 3) Responsible decision making, 4) Social interaction skills.

These SCS materials have been tested with teachers and students of all abilities and backgrounds in public, private, city, and suburban schools. The program has been successful due to the commitment of staff, ongoing support from leadership, and awareness that all student needs—emotional, social, and intellectual—must be met. The schools that had the most success with the program developed strong relationships with their students by infusing SCS principles into the culture of the school, rather than just using occasional add-on SEL or character education units. At these schools, teachers brought the activities to life by modeling desirable behaviors and creating an environment where all students felt safe, accepted, recognized, and celebrated for their individuality every day.

A Schoolwide Commitment

To improve classroom and school climate, the SCS materials can be used by an individual teacher or by an entire school or district. Either approach will work, but a systemic change can be realized only when an entire school makes a commitment to become a safe and caring place. By choosing the schoolwide approach, a school has the benefit of teamwork and support from all staff, plus parents and community members. Through the common language of clear expectations, consistency of messages, modeling of desirable behavior, and the use of vocabulary that will help everyone communicate more effectively, you will be able to create positive systemic change in your school.

To implement a schoolwide SCS program:

- Include social and emotional learning in your mission statement.
- Establish clear expectations for positive behavior.
- Be consistent with expectations and consequences.
- Establish a yearlong plan to reinforce parent involvement.
- Create a support system for all students, staff, and parents.
- Coordinate communication among all staff, including teachers, specialists, administrators, counselors, support staff, substitute teachers, and aides.
- Plan opportunities to recognize and celebrate successes.

Although classroom teachers are the primary implementers of the SCS lessons, administrators, counselors, social workers, health teachers, and other staff can be actively involved in the effort to infuse SEL into all areas of the school. Creating a schoolwide program takes thought and planning, but it's well worth the effort.

What Can Be Done About Bullying? Beyond Policy and Procedures

An essential goal of the SCS program is to create clear schoolwide and classroom expectations about bullying and its consequences. Ultimately, it is the responsibility of adults to create an environment where students feel protected once they report bullying as they witness or experience it. If adults are not consistent with this protection, students will quickly learn to either take matters into their own hands or remain silent.

- Establish a coordinated plan where staff, parents, and students work together to respond to bullying in a proactive and timely manner. Help parents understand the seriousness of this issue and give them the tools to help their children along the way.
- Provide ongoing training and support for all adults to teach them how to respond when they witness or hear about bullying behavior, and how to provide timely follow-up.
- Administer a survey to students to help you assess bullying behavior in your school and to find out if your students know where bullying takes place and how and where they can go for help.
- Set clear guidelines for coaching and supporting students who have been bullied as well as students who bully others if you wish to create systemic change.

Create a safe environment where students are encouraged to become positive bystanders. By creating a climate that encourages students to become positive bystanders and report bullying, you'll be sending a message to students that bullying is taken seriously in your school. Middle school students often report that while they don't like witnessing bullying behavior, they don't know how to help without getting themselves in trouble. Students also share that they choose not to get involved out of fear they will be bullied, excluded, or isolated by the kids who bully. Along with your support, give students clear strategies while always keeping their personal safety in mind.

- Ask for help from an adult you know and trust.
- Reach out to the student who is being bullied.
- Ask the bully to stop only if you feel safe and are not alone.
- Refuse to join the bully; don't laugh or encourage the situation.
- Do not look the other way when someone is in trouble.
- Break the silence about bullying with help from your friends and adults.

PART 2

Content Overview

Students learn best when they see how what they are learning will impact their lives. The more your students can relate to a situation through experiential activities, the more interest they will show in the lesson and the easier it will be for them to apply the skills in real-life situations. This Safe & Caring Schools resource guide includes activities that enable students to have conversations, to learn through inquiry, and to feel empowered to change their own behavior and contribute to the creation of a positive classroom and school culture.

SCS MONTHLY THEMES

The SCS materials provide a sequenced, yet flexible program for social and emotional learning (SEL). Activities are grouped into nine units, one for each month of the typical school year. A theme is designated for each month, so all grade levels using the program have the same monthly theme. This allows each grade level in a schoolwide program to use its specific age-appropriate activities to support the common theme throughout the school. The SCS monthly themes are the following:

- -

SEPTEMBER: Me and My School Community

OCTOBER: Discovering Our Feelings

NOVEMBER: My Support System

DECEMBER: Respect Yourself and Others

JANUARY: Bullying

FEBRUARY: Teaming Up for Success

MARCH: Conflict Resolution

APRIL: The Power to Choose

MAY: Follow Your Dreams

- -

Each SCS monthly theme is presented in a brief overview with social emotional definitions and key objectives to help focus the teaching. The theme is developed with a broad range of literature-based teaching activities, complete with reproducible activity sheets for the students. For easier printing of the activity sheets, they are also available on the CD-ROM included with this book. See pages 12–13 for the "Year-at-a-Glance" chart of all the activities within each monthly theme.

LITERATURE BASE

The SCS activities use literature to introduce key concepts, facilitate discussion, and lead into the activities. Using the books promotes active listening, helps increase comprehension, and motivates students to express themselves. The literature connections directly integrate SEL into core academics, making it easy for teachers to "build in" rather than "add on" SCS practices. Check your classroom, school library, or local public library for the books, or acquire some of the titles to start building an SEL library to share with all classrooms. When a suggested book is not available to you, consider another book of your own choosing or simply discuss the key concept of the book as it is described in the lesson plan.

LESSON PLANS

Each activity is presented with simple directions that include the "Learning Objectives," the "Materials Needed," and a five-part teaching plan: "***CHECK IT,***" "***READ IT,***" "***DO IT,***" "***TALK ABOUT IT,***" and "***WRITE ABOUT IT.***" In "Check It," the teacher finds out what the students already know about the subject and introduces the vocabulary. In "Read It," the students either read a text alone or are read a selection relating to the topic. "Do It" provides instructions for using the lesson's activity sheet. In "Talk About It," the teacher facilitates discussion on how the reading and activity relate to each other, and how the topic connects to students' lives. Finally, students respond in their journals to a specific prompt in "Write About It." From this, teachers will be able to discern how well the students internalize the lesson and determine if it needs to be revisited. Some activities include an additional section titled "More Cool Reads" that offers suggestions for further reading related to the topic.

The activities are designed to be used as starting points to introduce the key concepts of a safe and caring school. With open conversation, kids will gain a better understanding of the concepts and a sense of ownership of their own growth. See pages 12–13 for the "Year-at-a-Glance" chart of all the activities within each monthly theme.

INTEGRATED ACTIVITIES

In addition to the more than 100 lesson plans, ideas for integrating each monthly theme across curricular areas—language arts, literature, social studies, art, music, math, and science—are provided to follow up and expand on topics.

ASSESSMENT

Best practices include ongoing assessment for program mastery. The final activity sheet for each month is a short quiz to assess the students' grasp of the concepts related to the monthly theme. Three types of questions and a writing activity are included. You may choose to use a quiz as a pre- and post-test to demonstrate where students started and how far they have grown by unit's end.

YEAR-ROUND ACTIVITIES

To support the success of a schoolwide effort, a set of activities that can be implemented at the start of the school year and used throughout the year is included (pages 7–9). These activities provide the school with a common vision and language that will maximize the benefits of the SCS program.

SCS Implementation Plan

The SCS activities have been successfully used in home-rooms, in regular classroom settings, during advisory time, and in various youth or club programs.

Classroom teachers are commonly the primary implementers of the SCS lessons. Materials can be used independently in each classroom, but for systemic change, schools should consider a building-wide program. When all school staff—including teachers, administrators, counselors, social workers, media specialist, aides, coaches, and support staff—are involved in supporting the program, the students benefit from consistency of message and modeling of positive behavior. Schoolwide implementation creates an environment where students know what is expected of them, no matter where they are or what activities they are involved in throughout the day. To support the success of schoolwide implementation, it is essential for all staff to understand the philosophy of the SCS program—its goals, objectives, and action plan—and to be committed to working as a team to create a safe and caring school.

Counselors and social workers can use the program in small, student support groups during the school day, as part of after-school activities, or for parent presentations. In one-on-one situations, the activities can be used to practice specific skills, such as being assertive, using "I-messages," or diffusing negative situations. We have observed counselors and social workers playing a leadership role in promoting a comprehensive approach in the way SCS is used by all staff.

Media specialists and librarians have supported the schoolwide monthly theme by selecting appropriate reading and audiovisual materials for classes. Students can read the books and discuss how the characters feel, express their emotions, deal with conflict, and resolve problems.

An SCS library corner can be set up so staff and students know which books to read to support the theme of each month. Social studies, writing, and art teachers can provide support with SCS theme-based projects.

The Essential Role of Leadership

Children look to the adults around them for guidance, support, and safety. As the leaders of your school and classroom communities, you set the tone for the school year. To create a safe and caring school and achieve long-term positive change, the following strategies are recommended:

In a schoolwide program:

- **Mission.** Identify creating a safe and caring school as a schoolwide goal.

- **Core Team.** Assign a group to oversee the SCS program to keep implementation on track. The core team may be teachers from each grade level or a combination of teachers, administrators, support staff, specialists, and parents.

- **Action Plan.** Create and communicate an implementation plan to all staff, parents, and the community. Keep the lines of communication open so everyone has a voice.

- **Professional Development.** Use training and department planning to enhance the instructional process and effectively use new materials. Plan to train new teachers each year in the SCS program through in-service and teacher mentoring. Provide ongoing support, positive feedback, and a chance to celebrate progress.

- **Comprehensive Approach.** Fully integrate SEL into the daily curriculum and the daily life of students and teachers.

In the classroom:

- **Clear Expectations.** Have students help you create the classroom rules. Their active involvement will lead to positive engagement.

- **Follow Through.** Let students know you are committed to making sure everyone feels safe and has the right to learn and enjoy being in your classroom. Following through shows them you mean what you say.

- **Connect with Each Child.** Get to know your students at the beginning of the year. This will help you build strong, trusting relationships. As you invest in them, they will invest in you.

- **No Tolerance.** Explain to students the meaning of no tolerance for violence, harassment, and negative behavior. Conflicts are a normal part of life, but bullying and harassing others in your safe and caring school are not.

Teaching Tips

There are no simple answers or quick fixes that will create the kind of school community you and your students will want to be a part of every day. But there are a number of things you can do to engage kids in the process of learning to get along with others and accepting responsibility for their own actions. Here are a few suggestions.

BEST PRACTICES

Because the SCS materials are group-graded, plan to meet regularly (at least monthly) with all the teachers using the same book to determine which activities everyone will use. You may want to use some activities at all grade levels to support the schoolwide program, while reserving others for a specific grade level. Keep in mind that some repetition of activities is a good thing because it aids in learning and reinforcing key concepts. To be successful, your planning efforts need to be intentional and organized.

You can take several steps to help make the SCS program successful:

- Become familiar with the material. Review this resource guide in its entirety prior to using it.

- Be flexible. Use your creativity and knowledge to adapt the activities to meet the needs of your students.

- Be positive. Motivate and inspire your students.

- Diversify your teaching style. This SCS resource guide provides you with a diverse range of activities that enable you to work with multiple learning styles.

- Develop a cohesive group of students. Use small groups and pairs of students to complete many of the activities. Vary the way groups are formed—try counting off; odd and even numbers; using colors of clothes, shoes, eyes, or hair; alphabetical order; height; letting students choose (be sensitive to problems of exclusion), or other creative ways.

When lessons have personal meaning to students, they are more likely to change their behavior because they want to, rather than because they are told to do so. To motivate your students and make the lessons personal, keep these best practices in mind:

- Help students understand the new skills and why they matter to them.

- Demonstrate what the new skill looks like, sounds like, and feels like.

- Create opportunities for students to practice their new skills.

- Consider the use of journal writing to help kids personalize their new skills.

- Use teachable moments to correct and redirect students.

- Celebrate the students who adopt desirable behaviors in school.

- Model the new social and emotional skills as often as possible.

- Infuse SEL into academic subject areas.

PARENT INVOLVEMENT

Involve parents and guardians in the SCS process. Once you establish your classroom and school expectations, send a copy of them to the parents and guardians of all students. Enclose a short letter explaining how the SCS program works in your classroom and school. Explain that you are actively teaching social and emotional skills along with academics, and include the advantages of doing so. Ask for their support to help their kids practice the same expectations and skills at home for reinforcement and consistency. Keep the parents actively involved—send home tips, ideas, success stories, and pictures from events at your safe and caring school. Encourage parents to visit your school to help with specific activities.

ADVISORY/CLASSROOM MEETINGS

Misunderstandings at school, teasing, bullying, or use of inappropriate language can turn into big problems that take time away from teaching. Be proactive by using advisory time or classroom meetings to address these issues. By doing so, you create a forum where students can share their feelings, as well as review, process, and discuss ways to positively resolve conflicts.

Advisory/classroom meeting time gives you the opportunity to get to know your students better and allows you to build stronger relationships. It helps you create a natural peer support group, giving them a safe time and place to ask for help. Students have the opportunity to practice listening, taking turns, sharing feelings, showing empathy for others, problem solving, and making decisions. Explain to your students the purpose of this time and establish clear expectations so students feel safe to participate. You may want to start with these instructions:

- Use active listening.
- Wait for your turn to speak.
- Don't use put-downs.
- Respect everyone's feelings and ideas.
- It's okay to disagree.
- You have the right to pass.

Advisory time can be set up in different ways to meet the needs of your individual school plan. Although some schools rotate the time allocated for advisory during their academic lessons, most schools infuse about 20 minutes of advisory meeting time into daily homeroom activities. Other schools incorporate at least 40 minutes of advisory into homeroom three times a week, which allows teachers to take an activity to a deeper level and make it more meaningful for the students. The keys to the success of advisory time are setting clear expectations, maintaining consistency, and creating a safe place for students to have candid conversations and ask for support as they explore healthy ways to deal with daily challenges.

Morning advisory/classroom meetings give you a sense of how your students feel, which helps you set the tone for the day. Ask your students to share something that is happening in their world. This is also a good time to review your expectations and give students a quick preview of the day's activities.

Midday advisory/classroom meetings work well for students who return from lunch or special events with complaints or hurt feelings. When these feelings are not addressed, they can contribute to the students' inability to focus on the academic subjects.

End-of-the-day advisory/classroom meetings cover unfinished business, review the day, celebrate accomplishments, and remind students that you look forward to seeing them the next day. Students who leave school feeling isolated, hurt, threatened, or bullied on a regular basis often choose to skip school. Providing a safe environment for sharing feelings and resolving conflicts in a timely fashion will help the students feel secure and ready to come back the next day. It takes only one caring adult to make a difference in a student's life.

Emergency advisory/classroom meetings give you the time you need to confront issues as they happen so you can go back to teaching and students can complete their day without interference. The key is to be proactive and redirect your students before negative behaviors get out of control.

If students share too much personal information during advisory/classroom meetings, talk about the difference between private and public information. Take time to explain confidentiality and the importance of respecting each other's privacy. If a student refers to anything at home that sounds like an abusive situation, don't discuss it in class but talk privately with the student and bring it to the attention of the school administrator.

Year-Round Activities

You will want to implement some or all of these ideas and yearlong activities to build a positive school climate and create a safe and caring community for staff, students, and parents. Implementing these ideas at the start of the year and continuing to use them throughout the school year will support the common SCS vision, language, and expectations.

TEN IDEAS THAT WORK

1. Use grade level or department meetings to review expectations, rules, and support resources, and to discuss other topics related to SCS implementation.
2. Provide a monthly Ambassadors of Peace celebration (see page 8).
3. Decorate hallways and bulletin boards to promote your safe and caring school. Each month have a designated classroom display some of their completed activities.
4. Use morning announcements to communicate monthly themes and the monthly vocabulary (see first activity of each month).
5. In a parent newsletter, include the monthly theme with tips and ideas for home and family use.

6. Display the SCS Posters (available separately) in classrooms and throughout the school in common areas.
7. Have books related to the SCS themes featured in the library or classrooms.
8. Involve the student council or other student groups in promoting the messages of being a safe and caring school.
9. Use peer teaching by having older students teach monthly activities to younger students through reading, writing, drama, or art.
10. Include school nurses, health teachers, and school resource officers in promoting safe and healthy choices.

AMBASSADORS OF PEACE

The "Ambassador of Peace" activity (page 32) recognizes students for making good choices, resolving conflicts in peaceful ways, and practicing their positive character skills. Use the "Ambassadors of Peace" poster to remind students of the skills they need to work on to support a safe and caring school.

To conclude each month's SCS activities, nominate one or two students per classroom as Ambassadors of Peace for practicing their skills of peacemaking, such as making good choices, being respectful, or helping others. Have classroom teachers, counselors, or students nominate students by describing their specific peacemaking attributes. Create an Ambassadors of Peace nomination form using this model:

> **SAFE & CARING SCHOOLS**
> ### AMBASSADOR OF PEACE NOMINATION
> Date_____
> I nominate _____
> as an Ambassador of Peace because_____
> _____
> _____ .
> Signed_____

Plan an Ambassadors of Peace celebration, which might be a classroom party, a schoolwide or department assembly, or a grade-level breakfast. Invite each nominee's family to attend the celebration. Follow up with phone calls to encourage parents, other family members, or friends to attend.

During the celebration, present the students with Ambassadors of Peace certificates, buttons, or pendants. Give parents a copy of the nomination form so they know why their children were chosen as Ambassadors of Peace. (For example, Marina is an excellent listener, a great friend, and helpful and respectful to everyone.)

You may choose to acknowledge the Ambassadors of Peace on the same day as a "Student of the Month" or other school celebration. This coordinates the two programs into an existing initiative, which may be easier than finding time for two things in a busy school calendar.

ADOPT A HALLWAY

Are transition periods a challenge on a daily basis? A positive way to deal with this issue is to make sure everyone becomes responsible for the safety and peace of your school. Assign a specific hallway area to students from each classroom. Create an Adopt a Hallway sign for students to use to designate their area, using this model:

> **SAFE & CARING SCHOOLS**
> ### ADOPT A HALLWAY
> This part of the hallway has been adopted
> by:_____
> _____
> _____
> _____
> _____

Have students write their names on the sign as a promise to do their best to keep peace in that area of the school. This is to teach students to be responsible for their own actions, while being accountable to each other.

CREATIVE JOURNAL WRITING

Using the monthly Safe & Caring themes, ask students to write about real life in their journals as often as possible. Social and emotional learning is most effectively internalized when students can personally relate to the information presented. Encourage students to share their entries (unless they are too personal) so they can learn from each other.

COMMUNITY PEACE GARDEN

To practice teamwork skills, listening and following directions, and taking responsibility, involve the students, parents, and community in creating a garden. The peace garden can be the place where individuals or groups go when they need a quiet moment or need to resolve an issue before it becomes a big conflict. This is a good project in which to involve parents, community volunteers, gardeners, garden shops, carpenters, and home supply stores for donated time, expertise, and materials.

Choose a spot—outside, inside, or both—for your garden. (If inside, use potted plants and indoor benches or chairs in the garden.) With some expert help, build wooden benches to place in the garden. Prepare the soil for planting. When it is ready, plant flowers, bulbs, trees, and shrubs. Decorate the area with rocks, and have the students paint words of peace on the rocks. (You could use words and phrases from the SCS themes.) Add posts in the garden that can be used to display posters with positive messages. As you work together on the garden, reinforce lessons of teamwork, cooperation, responsibility, caring, and nurturing. Don't forget to have a community celebration once your garden is complete. Work together to provide ongoing care for the garden.

COMMUNICATION BOX

Create a classroom mailbox and label it "Communication Box." With all you try to accomplish during the day, it is not always possible to recognize the emotions and address the concerns of your students in a timely manner. The communication box is a safe place where students can leave confidential messages for you when they need adult support. Go through the box at least once a day so you can decide the urgency and the type of support a student needs.

SCS Teacher Survey

Use the teacher survey (pages 10–11) at the beginning of the school year, during the year when you want to check your progress, and as a post-test at the end of the school year. Part 1 helps you monitor how often you include social and emotional learning as part of your academic routine. Part 2 gives you a sense of how safe students feel in school and if they use their social and emotional skills on a regular basis.

TEACHER SURVEY—PART 1
SCHOOL/CLASSROOM CLIMATE

Using the 1 to 5 scale, circle the response that best describes your actions and proficiency at this time.
1 = Consistently   2 = Often   3 = Occasionally   4 = Infrequently   5 = Never

1. I set clear expectations in my classroom.	1	2	3	4	5
2. I enforce classroom and schoolwide expectations.	1	2	3	4	5
3. I teach students about being accountable for their own actions.	1	2	3	4	5
4. I recognize my students for using their social and emotional skills by choosing them as Ambassadors of Peace.	1	2	3	4	5
5. I develop a sense of community in my classroom.	1	2	3	4	5
6. I use advisory/classroom meetings to review new ideas and to practice social and emotional literacy.	1	2	3	4	5
7. I use cooperative groups to reinforce teamwork and peer teaching.	1	2	3	4	5
8. I model and use teachable moments to reinforce social and emotional learning in the lessons I teach.	1	2	3	4	5
9. I teach social and emotional literacy by infusing activities from the Safe & Caring Schools resource guide.	1	2	3	4	5
10. I teach students strategies to help them deal with bullying behavior.	1	2	3	4	5
11. I teach students conflict resolution and problem-solving strategies.	1	2	3	4	5
12. I meet with other staff to discuss and plan schoolwide activities to reinforce social and emotional learning.	1	2	3	4	5
13. I seek support from my colleagues when problems arise in my classroom so I can solve them more effectively.	1	2	3	4	5
14. I assess the effectiveness of my efforts to include social and emotional learning in my daily teaching practice.	1	2	3	4	5
15. I connect with parents to be partners in teaching and supporting social and emotional learning at home as in school.	1	2	3	4	5

SKILLS FOR SCHOOL. SKILLS FOR LIFE.

TEACHER SURVEY—PART 2
SKILLS AND KNOWLEDGE

Using the 1 to 5 scale, circle the response that best describes your actions and proficiency at this time.
1 = Consistently   2 = Often   3 = Occasionally   4 = Infrequently   5 = Never

1. My students feel safe at school.	1	2	3	4	5
2. My students understand the school and classroom expectations.	1	2	3	4	5
3. My students follow the school and classroom expectations.	1	2	3	4	5
4. My students know how to ask for help.	1	2	3	4	5
5. My students use conflict-resolution skills to deal with problems.	1	2	3	4	5
6. My students identify and express their emotions appropriately.	1	2	3	4	5
7. My students use good manners.	1	2	3	4	5
8. My students show respect toward adults and students.	1	2	3	4	5
9. My students show empathy toward others.	1	2	3	4	5
10. My students appropriately deal with bullying behavior at school.	1	2	3	4	5
11. My students practice active listening.	1	2	3	4	5
12. My students demonstrate the ability to make good choices.	1	2	3	4	5
13. My students recognize their gifts and talents.	1	2	3	4	5
14. My students know how to set goals.	1	2	3	4	5
15. My students have positive dreams for the future.	1	2	3	4	5

SAFE & CARiNG SCHOOLS

SKILLS FOR SCHOOL. SKILLS FOR LIFE.

Year-at-a-Glance, Grades 6–8

Use this chart as a planning tool to review the concepts and topics for the school year. You will see that the activities support the monthly theme and there is a logical progression to the order of the themes. Of course, it is possible to adjust the order of the themes to better fit with your curriculum or with other schoolwide events. Be creative with your planning and teaching.

Along with your teaching colleagues, select the activities you will use in your classroom each month. For example, you may decide that each 6th-grade teacher will devote 30 minutes to the same activity on the same day, or within the same week. Since this is a group-graded resource guide, be sure you are involving all the appropriate teachers in the planning.

Also, you can use this chart to help you plan ahead to gather the books you want to use as the literature base for each activity. The suggested book for each activity is listed opposite the activity name. See the activity directions for additional literature suggestions.

THEME	ACTIVITY TITLE—LITERATURE CONNECTION	
September Me and My School Community	SCS Vocabulary Activities Cool Rules — *Rules* Cool Character — *Dinah for President* Bill of Rights — *If You Were There When They Signed the Constitution* Golden Rule — *The Golden Rule (Darling)* Walking the Golden Rule — *What Are My Rights?* Our School Community — *Respecting Our Differences*	Introducing Me! — *The Year of the Dog* Private versus Public — *Character Building Day by Day* "Very Private" Taking Charge of My School Year — *Making Every Day Count* "October 7" Ambassador of Peace — *Paths to Peace* What I Need at School — *Character Building Day by Day* "The New Guy" If I Were Teacher/Principal/Counselor for a Day — *Character Building Day by Day* "Wash and Wear" Quiz
October Discovering Our Feelings	SCS Vocabulary Activities Un-Mix It! — *Character Building Day by Day* "Summer Job" It's All Connected — *Too Stressed to Think?* "Emotional Stressors" Can You Predict? — *Too Stressed to Think?* "Stress and Your Brain" What Happens When I Get Angry? — *Too Old for This, Too Young for That!* "Dealing with Anger" Stop, Think, Choose — *Too Old for This, Too Young for That!* "When You're Not Getting Along"	Don't Push My Buttons! — *Character Building Day by Day* "Set of Wheels" Attitude Makes a Difference — *Making Every Day Count* "February 28," "November 2" The Anger Meter — *Making Every Day Count* "March 6," "April 20" I-Messages — *Too Old for This, Too Young for That!* "Being a Good Friend," "I-messages" Not Fair! — *The Cow of No Color* "The Cow of No Color," "The Sound of Work" Perfectly Imperfect — *Making Every Day Count* "April 21," "April 22" Quiz
November My Support System	SCS Vocabulary Activities My Support System — *People Who Care About You* "Caring School Climate" Do You Understand Me Now? — *Making Every Day Count* "January 21," "July 29" Stressing the Positive — *Too Stressed to Think?* "Stress 101" Stress Stoppers — *Stress Can Really Get on Your Nerves!* Who Is a True Friend? — *More If You Had to Choose, What Would You Do?* "Not Exactly"	Finding Your Friendship Factors — *More If You Had to Choose, What Would You Do?* "Instant Replay" Appreciate It! — *Character Building Day by Day* "Someone to Talk With" Help Department — *Too Stressed to Think?* "Get the Help You Need" Peer Pressure — *The Courage to Be Yourself* "Losing My Friends to Weed" So-Called Friends — *Character Building Day by Day* "The Tree and the Pond" Quiz
December Respect Yourself and Others	SCS Vocabulary Activities The Language of Respect — *Character Building Day by Day* "Super Smart" My Story of Acceptance — *Beethoven Lives Upstairs* Don't Blame Me! — *Character Building Day by Day* "The Sand Sculpture" Work It Out — *Character Building Day by Day* "For Giving" Believe Me! — *Character Building Day by Day* "Hairstyles"	Private Space — *Too Old for This, Too Young for That!* "Privacy" Get the Facts — *The Courage to be Yourself* "Nasty Girls" Good Manners — *Be the Best You Can Be* Compassion in Our Community — *Character Building Day by Day* "Tears at the Table" Everybody Is Welcome — *The Printer* Quiz

SAFE & CARING SCHOOLS®

SKILLS FOR SCHOOL. SKILLS FOR LIFE.

January
Bullying

SCS Vocabulary Activities
Cool Enough to Care — *Making Every Day Count* "August 6"
You and Me — *The Courage to Be Yourself* "Sticking with Your Own Kind"
Don't Judge a Book by Its Cover! — *Character Building Day by Day* "The Spider Project"
The Other P.O.V. — *Character Building Day by Day* "The Bully"
Sticks & Stones — *The Courage to Be Yourself* "Sticks and Stones"
Bully Survey — *The Courage to Be Yourself* "Beating the Bullies"

A Bully Is Someone Who... — *How to Handle Bullies, Teasers, and Other Meanies*, "What Makes Bullies and Teasers Tick?"
Advanced Bullyology — *Too Old for This, Too Young for That!* "Bully Busting"
It's Never Cool to Bully! — *Too Stressed to Think?* "Surviving the Social Scene"
Cyberbullying — www.stopcyberbullying.org
Not Funny! — *More If You Had to Choose, What Would You Do?* "The Jackson Four"
Quiz

February
Teaming Up for Success

SCS Vocabulary Activities
Team Building Brainstorm — *Character Building Day by Day* "The Next One's for Us"
Accountability Is Awesome! — *Character Building Day by Day* "Dinner Duties"
Cooperation Is Key — *Character Building Day by Day* "Scrapbook Group"
Tracking Your Team — *Character Building Day by Day* "Team Spirit"

Cooperation — *Character Building Day by Day* "The Secret Club"
Leadership & Me — *Character Building Day by Day* "The Book Club"
Team Spirit! — "Lessons from the Geese"
Deciding Together as a Team — *Making Every Day Count* "June 20," "December 22"
Verbal versus Nonverbal Communication — *Making Every Day Count* "April 19"
Quiz

March
Conflict Resolution

SCS Vocabulary Activities
All Ears — *The How Rude! Handbook of Friendship & Dating Manners for Teens* "Polite Listening"
Get the Story Right! — *Making Every Day Count* "February 7," "May 12"
Imagine That! — *Character Building Day by Day* "Speaking Up"
Keep Your Cool — *Fighting Invisible Tigers* "Stand Up for Yourself"
Problem Solving Steps — Gandhi

Problem Solving Quiz — *Life Lists for Teens* "10 Tips for Solving Almost Any Problem"
It's Okay to Disagree — *Character Building Day by Day* "Agreeing to Disagree"
Conflict Inside Ourselves — *Character Building Day by Day* "Hanging Out with the Big Guys," "Talking to Myself"
What to Do About Conflict — *Too Old for This, Too Young for That!* "When You're Not Getting Along"
Stop, Think, Choose a Solution — *Life Lists for Teens* "8 Steps to Conflict Resolution"
Quiz

April
The Power to Choose

SCS Vocabulary Activities
I Have the Power to Choose — *Too Stressed to Think?* "Tool #4: Choosing"
Targeting Good Choices — *Too Stressed to Think?* "You Still Have Choices"
Who Is in Charge of You? — *Character Building Day by Day* "The Big Eraser"
Making Positive Choices — *The Courage to Be Yourself* "It Ain't Easy Being Hard"

Wheel of Choices — *The Courage to Be Yourself* "Lighten Up on Heavy People"
Learning from Our Choices — *Stick Up for Yourself!* "Make Choices"
Choice Week — *If You Had to Choose, What Would You Do?*
Think Before You Act — *Life Lists for Teens* "4 Steps to Feeling Peaceful"
Making a Difference at Our School — *Making Every Day Count* "April 27"
Making Wise Choices — *Making Every Day Count* "July 25"
Quiz

May
Follow Your Dreams

SCS Vocabulary Activities
My Gifts & Talents — *You Can Do It!*
I Can Do Anything! — *Amelia Earhart*
Which Way Will I Go? — *145 Things to Be When You Grow Up*
Positive Role Models — *Christopher Reeve: Actor and Activist*
Job Pictionary — *If You Could Be Anything, What Would You Be?*

Go for It! — *What Do You Really Want?* "The Goal-Getter Action Plan"
Stick to It! — *What Do You Really Want?* "Goal-Getters in Action"
My Dreams & Wishes — *What Do You Really Want?* "What Is a Goal?"
Self-Discipline — *Wilma Unlimited*
How I Did This Year — *What Do You Really Want?* "Reward Yourself"
Quiz

SEPTEMBER
Me and My School Community

- **Setting Expectations**
- **Classroom Community**
- **Social Awareness**
- **Self-Awareness and Acceptance**
- **Belonging**

Monthly Objectives

Students will:

- learn about and participate in setting up a safe and caring classroom community
- understand they are unique and learn to recognize, empathize with, and respect the individuality and diversity of others
- experience the importance of inclusion, belonging, and celebrating their families

Social Emotional Definitions

Acceptance: Willingness to treat someone as a member of a group.
Awareness: The ability to notice what is going on in the world around you.
Belonging: Being accepted in a place or a community.
Commitment: A promise to do something.
Community: A group of people who live or spend time in the same area and who may have common interests or backgrounds.
Equality: Treating all people fairly.
Expectations: Standards of behavior or performance.
Motivation: A feeling of enthusiasm that inspires you to take action.
Rules: Expectations to perform in a certain way.

TEACHING TIPS

- Setting clear expectations and teaching students how to interact with one another are important steps to learning how to get along.
- It is essential to define the desirable and expected behavior of your students.
- Students thrive when they know that who they are, what they say, and what they do matters to their teachers. Recognize them for their efforts to do well academically and socially.

In addition to the specific lesson plans for this month, you can use these optional ideas to integrate and extend the Safe & Caring themes into daily routines and across the curricular areas.

LANGUAGE ARTS

- Students create a genealogy tree and develop an appreciation for their families. Be aware of any adopted children or those who have lost parents.

- Students write stories that describe their uniqueness. During the month, students take turns reading their stories during advisory or writing block.

LITERATURE

- Students read *Laws* by Zachary A. Kelly to help them understand how laws are made and enforced. Discuss the benefits of having and following laws and rules.

- Go to the library. Have students choose books for independent reading that demonstrate individuality. Plan a Book Review Day. Students take turns being a book critic, sharing the book they read.

SOCIAL STUDIES

- Students read "The Children's Bill of Rights" created in 1996 by a group of children from around the world (http://web.kidlink. org/KIDFORUM/Bills/Rights.html). Discuss why this bill was created. Ask students if there are amendments they would like to add.

- Use a world map and push pins. Students show where their families or ancestors originated. Connect the pins with yarn, starting from the location of your school. This is a great way to introduce the concept of diversity.

ART

- Students read *No One Saw* by Bob Raczka, a book that encourages them to believe in themselves and to celebrate individuality. Kids learn how artists view the world in their own special way.

- *Dancing at the Louvre: Faith Ringgold's French Collection and Other Story Quilts*, a book by Dan

Cameron depicting Faith Ringgold's quilts, can be used to inspire students to create their own story quilts. Students begin a quilt project to research the ethnic and cultural diversity within the classroom or school.

- Create posters or murals showing ways all students can help make their school a safe and caring place.

MUSIC

- Students research songs dealing with celebration, community, respect, or individuality. Have them study the lyrics. Choose from these songs to add to your concert presentations. You might begin with: *Walt Disney World Millennium Celebration, Walt Disney Records,* 1999.

- *The Movement CD* by Greg Marshall and Jeremy Bryan, available through Free Spirit Publishing. Wholesome, positive hip-hop songs by the Figureheads explore the universal themes of making good decisions, discovering one's own voice, and celebrating the power of family and friendship.

MATH

- Prepare a Venn diagram showing the three basic communities students belong to: home, school, and neighborhood. Ask students: How are these communities alike and how are they different?

- Students read *If the World Were a Village: A Book About the World's People* by David J. Smith. Students learn about numbers while they gain a better understanding of how many people live on our planet, how many languages are spoken, how much money is earned, who is educated, who has enough to eat, and much more.

SCIENCE

- Students research ways they can use recycling as a way to keep their school and neighborhoods clean and to build a sense of community. Explore the process of reusing recycled material. Make paper with your students to demonstrate paper recycling.

Safe & Caring Vocabulary and Word Find

LEARNING OBJECTIVES

Students will:

- be introduced to vocabulary that supports learning how they should behave in a safe and caring classroom and school
- internalize the vocabulary as they use it throughout the month and year in real-life situations

MATERIALS NEEDED

"Safe & Caring Vocabulary" (page 22) and "Safe & Caring Word Find" (page 23) activity sheets, dictionaries, and pencils

LESSON PLAN

Use the vocabulary activities to introduce the concepts and common language associated with this month's theme. Throughout the month, use the words in writing, spelling, storytelling, and dealing with conflict situations.

For "Safe & Caring Vocabulary," explain how to use the secret code to decipher the message. (Our **_classroom_ _community_** has **_rules_** to help us establish a **_respectful_** and **_safe_** place where we can **_learn_** and **_grow_**. When we have the **_commitment_** of **_everyone_** in the group to **_communicate_** and **_act_** in **_positive_** ways, we **_create_** a place where every person feels **_accepted_** and **_appreciated_**. **_Together_**, we can overcome **_conflict_** and **_problems_**, **_explore_**, have **_fun_**, and **_discover_** our abilities and **_talents_**.)

For "Safe & Caring Word Find," discuss what the words mean after completing the page. You may want students to work in pairs to help each other.

For an added challenge, at the end of each month, have students work individually or in small groups to create their own word find puzzles, using the words defined in "Social Emotional Definitions" (see page 14).

Cool Rules

LEARNING OBJECTIVES

Students will:

- learn the importance of having rules and help create rules for their classroom community
- learn what behaviors are expected of them at school and school events

MATERIALS NEEDED

The book *Rules* by Cynthia Lord, "Cool Rules" miniposter (page 24), pencils or pens, and dictionaries

LESSON PLAN

CHECK IT   Students define *rules*, *expectations*, and *consequences* and discuss why we need rules at home, school, and in the community. Ask students: What would happen if people did not follow rules?

READ IT   Read *Rules*. Catherine has conflicting feelings about her younger brother, David, who is autistic. While she loves him, she also is embarrassed by his behavior. In an effort to keep life on an even keel, Catherine creates rules for him (for example, it's okay to hug Mom but not the clerk at the video store).

DO IT   Review the "Cool Rules" miniposter.

TALK ABOUT IT   Students talk about the type of classroom and school community they would like to be part of this year (*safe, inclusive, fun, creative, respectful, accepting, etc.*) and discuss the rules and expectations necessary to ensure a safe and caring classroom. Ask students: How are rules made and why? What are the consequences of breaking rules? Who is responsible for creating a safe and respectful school environment? Are the "Cool Rules" exclusive to your safety as individuals? How can you help each other follow the rules and expectations of your school or classroom?

WRITE ABOUT IT   In their journals, students respond to the prompt: What are the easiest and toughest rules to follow? Why?

Cool Character

LEARNING OBJECTIVES

Students will:

- gain a better understanding of the meaning of character by defining it and discussing how it contributes to making better choices
- identify people they admire because of their character traits

MATERIALS NEEDED

The book *Dinah for President* by Claudia Mills, "Cool Character" activity sheet (page 25), pencils or pens, and dictionaries

LESSON PLAN

CHECK IT Ask students to define *character*. Write the word *character* on the board and have students brainstorm a list of words that identify or relate to it. Ask students: What are the key character traits that help people coexist and get along? What positive character traits do we look for in friends and others around us? *(honesty, loyalty, integrity, respectfulness, fairness, responsibility, etc.)*

READ IT Read *Dinah for President*. Entering middle school, Dinah desperately wants to make a name for herself. She finds an answer to anonymity by running for class president.

DO IT Distribute and have students complete the "Cool Character" activity sheet. Working in pairs, students define *good character,* record each other's positive qualities, provide examples of people with good character, and explain how good character can help in life.

TALK ABOUT IT Students share in the large group what they learned about character. Have students introduce their partners and the positive character qualities they possess. Discuss who they chose as people of good character and why.

WRITE ABOUT IT In their journals, students respond to the prompt: A character trait I would like to work on is _____ because...

Bill of Rights

LEARNING OBJECTIVES

Students will:

- brainstorm and discuss ideas about how they can become positive citizens
- create a classroom or school Bill of Rights

MATERIALS NEEDED

The book *If You Were There When They Signed the Constitution* by Elizabeth Levy, pencils or pens, paper, markers, posterboard, and dictionaries

LESSON PLAN

CHECK IT Students define *promise, citizenship, community, equality, respect,* and *rights*. Form small groups and assign each group one of the words above to find in a dictionary. Introduce the importance of creating a safe school community. Ask students: How does creating a safe and respectful community relate to the Bill of Rights in the U.S. Constitution?

READ IT *If You Were There When They Signed the Constitution* contains basic facts of the framing of the Constitution in a series of questions and answers.

DO IT Students work in groups to create a Bill of Rights for the school or classroom community. Students brainstorm, discuss, and make a list of the rights they have as citizens of their school community. Create a Bill of Rights poster and display in the classroom.

TALK ABOUT IT Ask students: What did you learn about citizenship? What does it take to be a good citizen? Why is it important to have a Bill of Rights? Why did you choose each right in our classroom or school Bill of Rights? What did the founders hope to achieve when they created the original Bill of Rights? What can you personally do to be a good citizen of your school community?

WRITE ABOUT IT Another word for rights is *privileges*. In their journals, students respond to the prompt: How will my being a good citizen protect my rights and privileges and those of others in school and in my community?

MORE COOL READS *The Declaration of Independence* (Cornerstones of Freedom) by R. Conrad Stein describes the creation of said document. *The Bill of Rights* (Cornerstones of Freedom) by R. Conrad Stein discusses the first 10 amendments to the Constitution and the rights they are intended to protect.

Golden Rule

LEARNING OBJECTIVE

Students will:

- discuss the meaning of the golden rule and how it applies to everyday situations

MATERIALS NEEDED

The book *The Golden Rule* by Sandra Darling and Harold Darling, "Golden Rule" miniposter (page 26), dictionaries, markers, and posterboard

LESSON PLAN

CHECK IT Review the "Golden Rule" miniposter. Discuss the meaning of the golden rule. Have students define the words *dignity* and *respect*. Ask them: How do you show respect to others? How do you earn the respect of others? How do you recognize when someone shows respect? How do you feel when you are disrespected? What are some reasons people choose to show disrespect? Can people learn to care and be respectful?

READ IT *The Golden Rule* explores the golden rule, an ethical formulation that is found in some form in most of the world's religions. Included are many of the different ways the rule is expressed by both religious and secular thinkers.

DO IT Students work cooperatively in groups to create a poster showing how the golden rule can be used to create a safe, respectful, and inclusive school environment.

TALK ABOUT IT Each group will present and explain their poster, which can be displayed in the classroom or around the school. Ask students: Have you ever treated someone unfairly? Have you ever been excluded by others? How did you feel about it? What did you choose to do?

WRITE ABOUT IT In their journals, students respond to the prompt: Describe the impact of treating others the way you want to be treated. What results can you expect?

MORE COOL READS *The Golden Rule* by Ilene Cooper is a great discussion starter. Teachers, parents, and religious leaders will welcome it as a clear introduction to an important subject.

Walking the Golden Rule

LEARNING OBJECTIVE

Students will:

- learn to apply the golden rule to their daily lives, treating others with dignity and respect

MATERIALS NEEDED

The book *What Are My Rights? 95 Questions and Answers About Teens and the Law* by Thomas A. Jacobs, "Golden Rule" miniposter from previous activity (page 26), "Walking the Golden Rule" activity sheet (page 27), and pencils or pens

LESSON PLAN

CHECK IT Ask students to share stories about real-life situations where people were not treated with dignity and respect. The goal for this activity is to stimulate students' thinking about why it is important to apply the golden rule in their daily lives.

READ IT *What Are My Rights?*, "You and School" (pages 29–53), deals with legal issues kids face every day at school.

DO IT Distribute and have students complete the "Walking the Golden Rule" activity sheet. Students explain in their own words why the golden rule is "golden," respond to questions, and rate situations.

TALK ABOUT IT Students share ideas and thoughts about ways they can personally use the golden rule and how treating others with dignity and respect will contribute to people getting along.

WRITE ABOUT IT In their journals, students respond to the prompt: One way I have used the golden rule in my life is...

Our School Community

LEARNING OBJECTIVES

Students will:

- learn the meaning of community
- learn to appreciate their individuality and accept the uniqueness of others

MATERIALS NEEDED

The book *Respecting Our Differences: A Guide to Getting Along in a Changing World* by Lynn Duvall, "Our School Community" activity sheet (page 28), pencils or pens, and dictionaries

LESSON PLAN

CHECK IT Students define the word *community* and discuss the importance of belonging to a safe community. Have students compare different communities (family, school, neighborhood, and classroom).

READ IT The thought-provoking questions found in the "Time Out" sections of *Respecting Our Differences* can be used by independent readers or as classroom discussion starters. The anecdotal material features young people who have experienced prejudice and are working alone or in groups to overcome it. It encourages young adults to take action.

DO IT Distribute and have students complete the "Our School Community" activity sheet. Students respond to several questions and statements about the school community.

TALK ABOUT IT Ask students: What did you learn about communities and how are you expected to act in each one? Are the same behaviors accepted in all communities?

WRITE ABOUT IT In their journals, students respond to the prompt: What does it mean to be a part of a classroom, school, or neighborhood community?

Introducing Me!

LEARNING OBJECTIVES

Students will:

- share information about themselves with their classmates
- learn to appreciate their uniqueness

MATERIALS NEEDED

The book *The Year of the Dog* by Grace Lin, "Introducing Me!" activity sheet (page 29), pencils or pens, and camera (optional)

LESSON PLAN

CHECK IT Ask students if they know what it means to be unique. Discuss the importance of uniqueness and invite students to brainstorm different ways that each of them is a unique individual *(things they like to do, books they like to read, hobbies and interests they have, their wishes, their beliefs, culture, character traits, etc.).*

READ IT In *The Year of the Dog*, readers follow Grace, an American girl of Taiwanese heritage, through the course of one year—The Year of the Dog—as she struggles to integrate her two cultures.

DO IT Distribute the "Introducing Me!" activity sheet and have students complete it with a partner. Create a classroom scrapbook entitled "We Are All Unique." Use a camera to take pictures of each student to add to the scrapbook. Make copies of the completed activity sheets prior to putting the originals in the book. It is helpful to have a quick reference of personal information about each of your students.

TALK ABOUT IT Once students complete the activity, gather in the large group and have them share what they learned about each other.

WRITE ABOUT IT In their journals, students respond to the prompt: One thing I learned about my classmates was...

Private versus Public

LEARNING OBJECTIVES

Students will:

- learn about private versus public information
- determine what is acceptable to share with others and what they should keep to themselves

MATERIALS NEEDED

The book *Character Building Day by Day* by Anne D. Mather and Louise B. Weldon, "Private versus Public" activity sheet (page 30), and pencils or pens

LESSON PLAN

CHECK IT Introduce new vocabulary: *private, public,* and *confidential.* Ask the class: Can you explain the difference between private and public information? Why would people choose to share some information but not all? How does one decide with whom to share private thoughts or information? Who are the people you trust the most to share how you feel about different situations, challenges, or your dreams?

READ IT Read *Character Building Day by Day*, "Very Private" (page 201). This short, one-page story is about a brother who wants to read his sister's diary and use what he finds to tease her.

DO IT Distribute and have students complete the "Private versus Public" activity sheet. Students rate the information as to whether it can be shared (public) or should not be shared (private). Students also must state whom they can tell.

TALK ABOUT IT Students share their completed activity sheets. Tell students that they should know the appropriate time to share and discuss information. Some information can be shared with everyone, some only with those we really trust, and some with only our family. It is important to be able to distinguish the difference. It is a matter of personal safety in some cases and nobody's business in others. Ask students: How does one know the difference?

WRITE ABOUT IT In their journals, students respond to the prompt: It is important to know the difference between private and public information because...

MORE COOL READS *Character Building Day by Day* by Anne D. Mather and Louise B. Weldon, "Clean at School" (page 55). Whose business is it that Isabel is messy? *Too Old for This, Too Young for That!* by Harriet S. Mosatche and Karen Unger, "Helping Friends with Their Feelings" (pages 70–71).

Taking Charge of My School Year

LEARNING OBJECTIVES

Students will:

- define *mission* and *vision*
- create a set of personal goals for the school year

MATERIALS NEEDED

The book *Making Every Day Count* by Pamela Espeland and Elizabeth Verdick, "Taking Charge of My School Year" activity sheet (page 31), pencils or pens, dictionaries, and envelopes for each student

LESSON PLAN

CHECK IT Part of a great education is learning how to succeed in life emotionally and socially, as well as academically. By encouraging students to set goals in each of these areas, we help them reach their full potential. Talk about the different types of goals students might have or wish to develop. Review social and emotional learning as compared to academic learning. Ask students: How are they alike and different?

READ IT *Making Every Day Count*, "October 7" (page 281) is a short reading that discusses life without goals.

DO IT Students define the words *mission (a particular task someone believes is important to carry out)* and *vision (what one would like to see happen in the future)*. Complete the "Taking Charge of My School Year" activity sheet. After students are done, have them put their activity sheets into envelopes labeled with their names. Collect the envelopes and store in a place where students can refer to them throughout the year to see if they accomplished their goals.

TALK ABOUT IT Students share their ease or difficulty in creating goals for themselves. Explain that part of being in charge of their own destiny is having a plan, a set of goals, and people who can help them achieve those goals. Remind students that you are one of the adults they can count on for support and encouragement as they take on new risks, or as they experience changes and concerns about meeting their goals during the school year.

WRITE ABOUT IT In their journals, students respond to the statements: One long-range goal of mine is _____. Short-range goals that might help me get there are _____.

Ambassador of Peace

LEARNING OBJECTIVES

Students will:

- learn how to become Ambassadors of Peace
- learn how to be recognized on a monthly basis for using positive character skills

MATERIALS NEEDED

The book *Paths to Peace: People Who Changed the World* by Jane Breskin Zalben, copies of nomination forms (see page 8), "Ambassador of Peace" activity sheet (page 32) and pencils or pens

LESSON PLAN

CHECK IT Discuss what an Ambassador of Peace is and does. Review the "Ambassadors of Peace" poster if you purchased it (see page 200) and the nomination process. Describe how students will be recognized for their efforts to display positive character traits on a regular basis.

READ IT In *Paths to Peace,* one-page biographies profile 16 world peacemakers, ranging from Emerson, Gandhi, and Martin Luther King Jr., to Daw Aung San Suu Kyi, a political prisoner in Myanmar.

DO IT Distribute and have students complete the "Ambassador of Peace" activity sheet. Have students work with a partner to record ways they can support positive school climate change. Finish by creating commercials to inspire kids to become Ambassadors of Peace.

TALK ABOUT IT Students share the information from the completed activity sheets. Discuss specific skills students can use to contribute individually or as a group to make school a safe and caring place.

WRITE ABOUT IT In their journals, students respond to the prompt: To be an Ambassador of Peace, I need to...

What I Need at School

LEARNING OBJECTIVES

Students will:

- review how a safe and caring school looks, feels, and sounds
- determine how they can make their school safe and caring

MATERIALS NEEDED

The book *Character Building Day by Day* by Anne D. Mather and Louise B. Weldon, "What I Need at School" activity sheet (page 33), and pencils or pens

LESSON PLAN

CHECK IT   Have students share their ideas about what makes a school a safe and respectful place. Ask students: Do you have a sense of pride in your school? What are some reasons you feel proud to be part of your school community? What are some things you think need to be changed? What does it mean to be a "positive bystander"? Set the tone for the year by formulating expectations that support the idea of students and adults working together to create a safe and productive school environment.

READ IT   *Character Building Day by Day*, "The New Guy" (page 37) is about Tyrone, who is new at school. How does Derrek help him?

DO IT   Distribute and have students complete the "What I Need at School" activity sheet. Students record what they think works at school and what needs to be changed.

TALK ABOUT IT   Ask students: What is required from a school to have everybody get along? Is it possible? Why is it important to get to know people at school? What can you do to be more inclusive, especially with new students? What can be done to help make school a safe and fun place?

WRITE ABOUT IT   In their journals, students respond to the prompt: If I could change one thing about my school...

If I Were Teacher/Principal/Counselor for a Day

LEARNING OBJECTIVE

Students will:

- gain a better understanding of responsibility for themselves and others

MATERIALS NEEDED

The book *Character Building Day by Day* by Anne D. Mather and Louise B. Weldon, "If I Were Teacher/Principal/Counselor for a Day" activity sheet (page 34), and pencils or pens

LESSON PLAN

CHECK IT   This is an opportunity for students to explore and appreciate the many aspects of a teacher, principal, or counselor's daily routine. Ask students: What do these people do that make your days go more smoothly? In turn, what can you do to show appreciation for what they do each day? How can you and your friends help out by being responsible for your actions?

READ IT   Read *Character Building Day by Day*, "Wash and Wear" (page 217). Bennie blames his mom because he wore one blue and one black sock to school.

DO IT   Distribute the "If I Were Teacher/Principal/Counselor for a Day" activity sheet. Students first list their qualifications for the job of a temporary teacher, principal, or counselor, then create a plan of what to do with kids for an entire day. Encourage them to be creative but realistic about what they are capable of in a day.

TALK ABOUT IT   Students share their completed activity sheets. The goal is to help them gain a better understanding and appreciation of what it takes to plan, organize, and be responsible for the safety and well-being of others while creating a safe place where everyone can learn.

WRITE ABOUT IT   In their journals, students respond to the prompt: I need to take more responsibility for _____ in my life because...

Me and My School Community Quiz

To assess student progress, use the quiz on page 35.
(Answers: 1-F, 2-T, 3-F, 4-T, 5-F, 6-d, 7-d, 8-a, 9-community, everyone, 10-help, positive)

Safe & Caring Vocabulary

Use the code to spell the missing words.

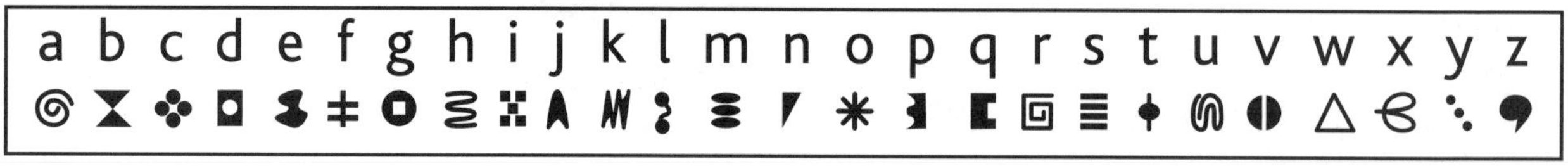

a	b	c	d	e	f	g	h	i	j	k	l	m	n	o	p	q	r	s	t	u	v	w	x	y	z

Our _ _ _ _ _ _ _ _ _ _ _ _ _ _ _ _ _ has _ _ _ _ _

to help us establish a _ _ _ _ _ _ _ _ _ _ and _ _ _ _

place where we can _ _ _ _ _ and _ _ _ _. When we

have the _ _ _ _ _ _ _ _ _ _ of _ _ _ _ _ _ _ _ in the

group to _ _ _ _ _ _ _ _ _ _ _ and _ _ _ in _ _ _ _ _ _ _ _

ways, we _ _ _ _ _ _ _ a place where every person feels

_ _ _ _ _ _ _ _ _ and _ _ _ _ _ _ _ _ _ _ _ _. _ _ _ _ _ _ _ _ _,

we can overcome _ _ _ _ _ _ _ _ and _ _ _ _ _ _ _ _ _,

_ _ _ _ _ _ _ _, have _ _ _ _, and _ _ _ _ _ _ _ _ our abilities

and _ _ _ _ _ _ _ _.

Define the word **inclusion**. _____

_____

_____

Write a sentence using the words **diversity** and **equality**.

_____

_____

_____

we are
a safe
& caring
school.

Safe & Caring WORD FIND

Find and circle the words listed at the bottom of the page.

(Hint: Answers can run forward, backward, up, down, or diagonally.)

U	P	P	O	S	I	T	I	V	E	Y	G	C
N	C	O	M	M	I	T	M	E	N	T	E	U
I	O	L	B	E	L	O	N	G	T	A	T	L
Q	M	A	G	M	U	Q	L	C	S	L	T	T
U	M	T	C	E	P	S	E	R	R	E	A	U
E	U	O	S	R	U	P	W	A	L	N	L	R
I	N	B	W	I	S	S	O	G	O	N	O	E
R	I	C	L	U	S	I	Q	U	N	S	I	M
S	C	G	R	S	W	L	U	O	S	I	M	E
C	A	R	F	N	G	F	W	L	F	M	A	E
H	T	F	F	R	I	E	N	D	S	I	O	T
O	I	A	E	M	U	S	A	O	F	L	L	S
O	O	M	L	T	O	T	U	B	W	A	D	E
L	N	I	S	U	Y	E	S	I	M	R	R	F
G	O	L	D	E	N	R	U	L	E	R	N	L
S	W	Y	C	O	M	M	U	N	I	T	Y	E
Q	A	G	D	I	V	E	R	S	I	T	Y	S
L	B	A	C	C	E	P	T	A	N	C	E	O

SAFETY	BELONG	CARING	INCLUSION
UNIQUE	POSITIVE	COMMITMENT	SCHOOL
COMMUNICATION	RESPECT	GOLDEN RULE	CULTURE
SELF ESTEEM	DIVERSITY	ACCEPTANCE	FRIENDS
COMMUNITY	SIMILAR	GET ALONG	FAMILY

we are
a safe
& caring
SCHOOL.

COOL RULES

In our class, we have the right to:

- Be safe.
- Be treated with respect.
- Be accepted for who we are.
- Agree to disagree.
- Share our feelings and ideas.
- Learn and be creative.
- Not be bullied.
- Stand up for what we believe in.

we are a safe & caring school.

COOL CHARACTER

At our Safe & Caring School we develop positive character.

What does having positive character mean to you?

_____
_____
_____
_____

Qualities you have

_____
_____
_____
_____
_____
_____

2-way interview

Qualities your friend has

_____
_____
_____
_____
_____
_____

Can you name some people with positive character? How can you tell?

How does having positive character help you at school and in life?

_____
_____
_____
_____
_____
_____
_____
_____

People in Sports

People in Entertainment

People in School

we are a safe & caring school.

From *Safe & Caring Schools® Grades 6–8* by Katia S. Petersen, Ph.D., copyright © 2008. Free Spirit Publishing Inc., Minneapolis, MN; www.freespirit.com. This page may be photocopied for individual, classroom, or small group work only. For other uses, call 800-735-7323.

GOLDEN RULE

Treat others the way you want to be treated...

...with dignity and respect!

WALKING THE GOLDEN RULE

What's so "golden" about the golden rule?

_____
_____
_____
_____
_____
_____
_____

What respect means to me...

How I want others to treat me...

When I am respectful, I choose to treat others...

 **Gold or Cold?**

Use a "G" or a "C" to score whether the situations below follow the golden rule.

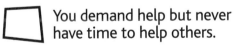 A friend is upset, and you take time to listen.

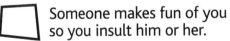 You demand help but never have time to help others.

☐ Someone makes fun of you so you insult him or her.

☐ While working on a group project, you try to make sure everyone shares the workload AND the credit.

 We are a safe & caring school.

To me, community means...

OUR SCHOOL COMMUNITY

A **safe school community** is important to me because...

Something I would like to change at our school is...

Things that make our school less safe, less caring, and less fun are...

Things I can do to make our school a safe and cool place...

Circle 10 positive things you find in a safe and caring school.

safety   conflict   lying
teasing   cooperation   yelling
friendship   fun   selfishness   rules

communication   interests
ignoring   hitting   excluding
respect   talents
bullying
commitment

we are a safe & caring school.

INTRODUCING ME!

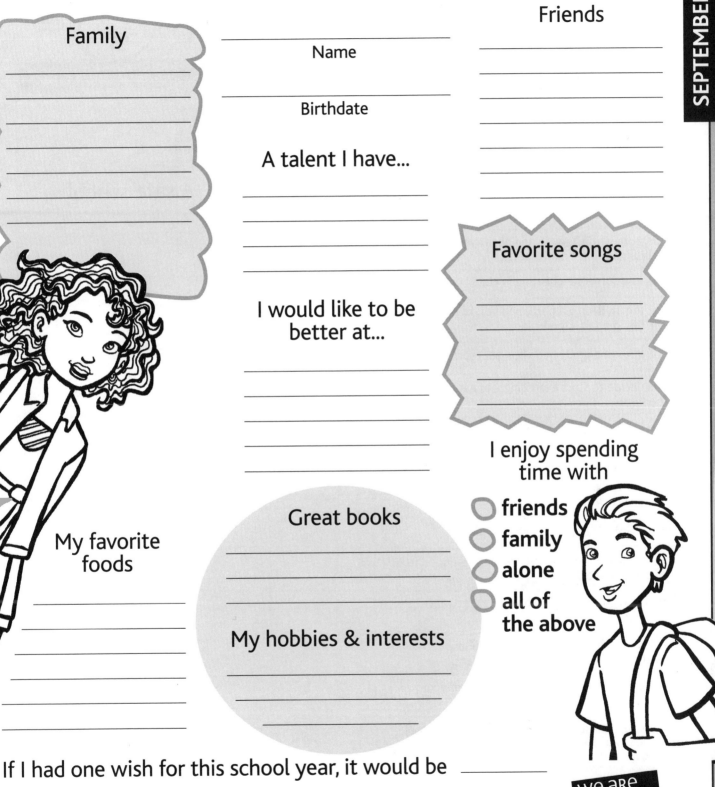

Family

Name

Birthdate

A talent I have...

I would like to be better at...

Friends

Favorite songs

I enjoy spending time with

○ **friends**
○ **family**
○ **alone**
○ **all of the above**

Great books

My hobbies & interests

My favorite foods

If I had one wish for this school year, it would be _____

PRIVATE VERSUS PUBLIC

Read the following situations and decide if it is information you should keep to yourself or if it is okay to share, and then check the appropriate box. If you can share it, write who you think you can share it with. Be prepared to explain your answers.

Situation	Don't share	Share	Share with who?
Your family just got a new car.			
You overheard a group of students talking about hurting someone after school.			
A classmate keeps asking to copy your homework.			
Your sister has a crush on someone and you think you know who.			
Someone you know posted negative photos of a classmate on the Internet.			
You saw someone cheating in class.			
You are invited to a party and you know there will be no adult supervision.			
You got good grades on your last report card.			
You decide to start exercising and eating healthy foods.			
You have two people who want to go with you to the school dance, but you can't decide who to choose.			
You see some kids bullying a student at the bus stop every day.			
Your family is taking a trip this summer.			
Someone asks for your personal information in an online chatroom.			
Your dad got a new job so you have to move away from friends.			
Kids you know are using their cell phones to send mean text messages to a student.			
You are being excluded from a group of your peers.			
You saw a kid steal a DVD from the movie store.			

TAKING CHARGE OF MY SCHOOL YEAR

Mission: To have a great year at school!

Vision: Write two goals and two steps to help achieve the goals.

Reflect: For each category below ask yourself:

1) Am I where I want to be?
2) Do I need help?
3) Who can help?

Academic Goals
1) _____
_____
_____
2) _____
_____
_____

Steps
1) _____
_____
_____
2) _____
_____
_____

Social Goals
1) _____
_____
_____
2) _____
_____
_____

Steps
1) _____
_____
_____
2) _____
_____
_____

Emotional Goals
1) _____
_____
_____
2) _____
_____
_____

Steps
1) _____
_____
_____
2) _____
_____
_____

we aRe
a safe
& caRiNG
SCHOOL.

An AMBASSADOR OF PEACE
is someone who...

_____

_____

_____

_____

As Ambassadors of Peace we can do the following to create a Safe & Caring School:

_____

_____

_____

_____

_____

_____

One thing I can do to make a positive difference in my school:

_____

_____

_____

_____

_____

_____

Create a Public Service Announcement or commercial to inspire and encourage students to become Ambassadors of Peace.

we aRe a SaFe & CaRiNG SCHOOL.

WHAT I NEED AT SCHOOL

Rules I'd like to see:

Things I can do to be a
positive bystander:

What students and adults can do to
create a safe and respectful community:

Things to learn about:

What I need in my school
environment to help me learn:

IF I WERE ☐ TEACHER FOR A DAY
☐ PRINCIPAL
☐ COUNSELOR

My Qualifications for the Job

My plan for the day...

Here's what I would do...

WE ARE a SAFE & CARING SCHOOL.

Me and My School Community Quiz

True or False (circle the correct answer)

1) I can't really take charge of my school year because the adults plan out everything............. **True / False**

2) Developing positive character and skills can help me face challenges better at school........ **True / False**

3) Respect is something others give you only if you are cool. .... **True / False**

4) Sometimes it helps to share private things with others, but it can be hard because you need to find someone you trust. .... **True / False**

5) The only thing I need to do to be responsible at school is show up......................... **True / False**

Multiple Choice (circle the correct answer)

6) In a Safe & Caring School:
   - **a.** caring isn't as important as being tough.
   - **b.** we respect and accept each other's differences.
   - **c.** we learn how to appreciate what our teachers do to help us grow.
   - **d.** b and c

7) The opposite of positive self-esteem is:
   - **a.** not giving yourself a chance to try new things.
   - **b.** ignoring how you feel when someone is unfair to you.
   - **c.** not getting help when you don't understand.
   - **d.** all of the above

8) Ambassadors of Peace help make our school safe and caring by:
   - **a.** being cool enough to help other kids out.
   - **b.** being bossy.
   - **c.** giving others a bad reputation by talking about the problems they cause.
   - **d.** none of the above

Fill in the Blanks

9) Our school c_____ includes e_____.

10) We can h_____ each other build p_____ character skills.

Real-Life Writing

To have a great year at school, describe ways you can take charge of your school year as well as help others.

OCTOBER
Discovering Our Feelings

- **Awareness and Appropriate Expression of Feelings**
- **Anger Management**

- **Problem Solving**
- **Assertiveness**

Monthly Objectives

Students will:

- identify and express their feelings appropriately through interactive activities and role play
- learn two strategies—"I-messages" and "Stop, Think, Choose"—to help them resolve conflicts in positive ways

Social Emotional Definitions

Anger Management: Dealing with your anger in a positive way.

Anxiety: Nervousness and worry about a situation with an uncertain outcome.

Attitude: An opinion about something that influences your actions.

Confidence: The belief in your ability to succeed.

Emotions: Feelings about something or somebody.

Integrity: The quality of being honest and doing the right thing.

Memories: Information you retain about past events and experiences.

Negotiation: Reaching an agreement with others through discussion and compromise.

Reality: The situations that actually exist or happen in day-to-day life.

Self-conscious: Feeling uncomfortable about your shortcomings and believing that others notice them as well.

TEACHING TIPS

- Provide students with a sense of belonging.
- Get to know your students.
- Teach students how to manage their anger.
- Build trusting relationships.
- Give students an opportunity to share something about themselves.

OCTOBER INTEGRATED ACTIVITIES

In addition to the specific lesson plans for this month, you can use these optional ideas to integrate and extend the Safe & Caring themes into daily routines and across the curricular areas.

LANGUAGE ARTS

- Students visit the library and choose a book about feelings. After reading the story, they write or draw a picture about the feelings they explored.
- Students visit the primary grades to read picture books about feelings.
- Students create a skit or a puppet show about feelings and stage a performance for younger students or parents.
- Students write about how the characters in the books they read could use I-messages to resolve their conflicts. They can rewrite the ending of the story and discuss in the large group.
- Television shows are full of emotions. Discuss a show students have already watched or choose a movie to watch in class. Students record which emotions the characters demonstrated. Ask students: How did the characters express their emotions?

LITERATURE

- Organize book review clubs. Students examine and give their expert opinions on the books they've read.
- Students create their own classroom book of short stories they write about feelings.
- Divide the class into small groups and give each group three or four letters of the alphabet. Students come up with as many feelings words as they can that start with those letters. When they complete their lists, all groups work together to create a Feelings Dictionary.

SOCIAL STUDIES

- Have students discuss attitudes people have toward different cultures, ideas, traditions, and customs.

ART

- Students create posters for the classroom that show different emotions.
- Students make an illustrated classroom book of feelings.
- Each student draws a self-portrait showing a specific emotion and writes guidelines for appropriate ways to express that feeling.

MUSIC

- Explore a variety of music and ask students to identify the different moods and emotions expressed in the music.
- Students write new lyrics for old songs that express different emotions than the original.

MATH

- Students tally the emotions they see expressed in their classroom community and graph them.
- Read *Famous Problems and Their Mathematicians* by Art Johnson (pages 41–43).

SCIENCE

- Read and do activities in *Psychology for Kids Vol. 2: 40 Fun Experiments That Help You Learn About Others* by J. Kincher.

Safe & Caring Vocabulary and Word Find

LEARNING OBJECTIVES

Students will:

- be introduced to vocabulary that supports learning about their feelings and understanding how emotions relate to their safe and caring classroom
- internalize the vocabulary as they use it throughout the month and year in real-life situations

MATERIALS NEEDED

"Safe & Caring Vocabulary" (page 43) and "Safe & Caring Word Find" (page 44) activity sheets, dictionaries, and pencils

LESSON PLAN

Use the vocabulary activities to introduce the concepts and common language associated with this month's theme. Throughout the month, use the words in writing, spelling, storytelling, and dealing with conflict situations.

For "Safe & Caring Vocabulary," students fill in the blanks with words from the word bank. (It is ***important*** to be ***aware*** of the ***emotions*** we ***experience*** and what we ***choose*** to do with them. ***Discovering*** our feelings is a significant ***journey***, because the more we learn to ***recognize*** how we feel, the more we ***understand*** ourselves. Some ***feelings*** are ***positive*** and others can make us ***uncomfortable*** and ***stressed***. Recognizing stress and knowing how to make the ***right choices*** is a ***healthy***, ***powerful*** step toward ***understanding*** how to ***communicate*** with ***people*** around us in a positive way.)

For "Safe & Caring Word Find," discuss what the words mean after completing the page. You may want students to work in pairs to help each other.

For an added challenge, at the end of each month, have students work individually or in small groups to create their own word find puzzles, using the words defined in "Social Emotional Definitions" (see page 36).

Un-Mix It!

LEARNING OBJECTIVES

Students will:

- learn to identify different kinds of feelings
- learn to empathize with others

MATERIALS NEEDED

The book *Character Building Day by Day* by Anne D. Mather and Louise B. Weldon, "Un-Mix It!" activity sheet (page 45), and pencils or pens

LESSON PLAN

CHECK IT   Review what it means to empathize. Tell students that feelings are an important part of who we are, because they are reactions to things that happen to us every day. Sometimes, though, our feelings get all mixed up. When that happens, it can be hard to say or do the right thing. When we learn to recognize and understand our own feelings, we are better able to empathize with others.

READ IT   Read *Character Building Day by Day*, "Summer Job" (page 62). Sam empathizes with the homeless.

DO IT   Distribute the "Un-Mix It!" activity sheet. Students unscramble the words and then write about one feeling that may have been confusing for them.

TALK ABOUT IT   Not all students feel comfortable sharing their feelings. Sometimes they don't believe they matter to anyone. Emphasize to students that teachers are there to help them. Review the list of feelings as a class. Ask students: What other feelings do you experience? Take a count of the most common feelings students have and the different ways they choose to express them. Discuss how students can recognize the feelings of others by listening to tone of voice, observing body language, and paying attention to actions.

WRITE ABOUT IT   In their journals, students respond to the prompt: Describe a time when a friend needed someone to empathize and you were there. How did you help?

It's All Connected

LEARNING OBJECTIVES

Students will:

- learn that thoughts, emotions, attitudes, and actions are all connected
- learn how they feel in different situations and how their choices affect their actions

MATERIALS NEEDED

The book *Too Stressed to Think?* by Annie Fox and Ruth Kirschner, "It's All Connected" activity sheet (page 46), and pencils or pens

LESSON PLAN

CHECK IT Ask students: What are emotions? What outside circumstances can cause them to change? Has anyone ever experienced roller coaster emotions? Why do you think this happens?

READ IT *Too Stressed to Think?*, "Emotional Stressors" (page 12) lists stressors students might experience.

DO IT Distribute and have students complete the "It's All Connected" activity sheet. Students respond to certain situations with thoughts, feelings, attitudes, and actions.

TALK ABOUT IT Students often find themselves dealing with tough choices or difficult situations. Discuss how to make the connection between their feelings and their attitude about a situation and/or people. Talk about empathy and how to recognize the feelings of others. Ask students: Why is empathy important? How will it affect your situations?

WRITE ABOUT IT In their journals, students respond to the prompt: Have you ever jumped to conclusions about things people have said to you? What did you do or what can you do to communicate your true feelings in a respectful way?

MORE COOL READS *My Feelings Are Like Wild Animals! How Do I Tame Them?* by Gary Egeberg. Practical, simple ways to improve one's emotional life.

Can You Predict?

LEARNING OBJECTIVE

Students will:

- explore the connection between their emotions and their reactions to different situations

MATERIALS NEEDED

The book *Too Stressed to Think?* by Annie Fox and Ruth Kirschner, "Can You Predict?" activity sheet (page 47), and pencils or pens

LESSON PLAN

CHECK IT Everyone reacts to stressful situations in different ways depending on the feelings they experience. Some people want to share their feelings with someone right away, some need privacy and quiet time to think, while others let their feelings come out like a huge explosion. Ask students: How do you respond to stress?

READ IT *Too Stressed to Think?*, "Stress and Your Brain" (pages 18–21) explains why teens react the way they do at times.

DO IT Distribute and have students complete the "Can You Predict?" activity sheet. Students describe how they might react to real-life situations dealing with their family, friends, school, and neighborhood.

TALK ABOUT IT Ask students: What do we mean by *prediction*? Have you ever reacted to a situation before thinking? What happens if you take a moment to think before reacting? Is it possible to predict what might happen? Do you wish you had taken time to think before you did or said something? How can these situations be corrected?

WRITE ABOUT IT In their journals, students respond to the prompt: Write about a time when you felt angry or upset and you treated someone unfairly.

What Happens When I Get Angry?

LEARNING OBJECTIVES

Students will:

- gain a better understanding of what happens to their bodies when they feel angry
- learn about impulse control, choices, and consequences

MATERIALS NEEDED

Too Old for This, Too Young for That! by Harriet S. Mosatche and Karen Unger, "What Happens When I Get Angry?" activity sheet (page 48), and pencils or pens

LESSON PLAN

CHECK IT Ask students which feelings they think are okay for people to have and express. Remind students that *all*

feelings are important, including anger, but it is never okay to hurt others emotionally or physically just because we feel upset or angry. As a class, brainstorm a list of negative and positive choices people make about how to express their anger.

READ IT   *Too Old for This, Too Young for That!*, "Dealing with Anger" (pages 66–67) describes anger and ways to deal with it.

DO IT   Distribute the "What Happens When I Get Angry?" activity sheet. First, students review the signs of anger. Ask students: Can you think of others? Next, students circle the choices they have used to help them calm down and add some of their own.

TALK ABOUT IT   Students share what works best to calm down when they are angry. Point out that what works for one person might not work for another. Ask students: Who in the group needs to be left alone? Who needs to be active to blow off some steam? Who needs to process their feelings out loud? Share daily situations where students might get frustrated or upset. Ask students: What can you do to prevent making negative choices? Counting to 10 can help, but it is only part of the solution. Make sure students realize they can take the time they need to calm down before reacting, but resolutions are still needed.

WRITE ABOUT IT   In their journals, students respond to the prompt: A time I responded poorly to a situation because I was angry was...

  MORE COOL READS   *A Guys' Guide to Anger, A Girls' Guide to Anger* by Hal Marcovitz and Gail Snyder.

Stop, Think, Choose

LEARNING OBJECTIVES

Students will:

- learn about conflict
- learn a method to help them stay calm and resolve conflicts in a positive way

MATERIALS NEEDED

The book *Too Old for This, Too Young for That!* by Harriet S. Mosatche and Karen Unger, "Stop, Think, Choose" mini-poster (page 49), paper, and pencils or pens

LESSON PLAN

CHECK IT   Write the words *conflict* and *impulse control* on the board. Ask students: What do the words mean and how are they related? Conflict is a natural part of life, though often not a pleasant part. Ask students: How hard is it to deal with conflict situations when you are upset?

READ IT   *Too Old for This, Too Young for That!*, "When You're Not Getting Along" (pages 102–105).

DO IT   Students review the "Stop, Think, Choose" mini-poster in small groups and make a list of conflict situations in their lives.

TALK ABOUT IT   Students share times of conflict when it was difficult for them to stop and think before they reacted. Discuss the concept of consequences, both positive and negative, and what it means to take responsibility for your actions.

WRITE ABOUT IT   In their journals, students respond to the prompt: Three things I can choose to do when I feel angry are...

Don't Push My Buttons!

LEARNING OBJECTIVES

Students will:

- identify what makes them angry and how they respond to it
- explore the connection between the brain and emotions

MATERIALS NEEDED

The book *Character Building Day by Day* by Anne D. Mather and Louise B. Weldon, "Don't Push My Buttons!" activity sheet (page 50), and pencils or pens

LESSON PLAN

CHECK IT   Ask students: Can you explain the phrase "don't push my buttons"? Discuss how each of us may react differently to the same situation. Why would that be? Do we all have different levels of tolerance?

READ IT   In *Character Building Day by Day*, "Set of Wheels" (pages 11–12), Barry is angry with his sister for causing him to be late for practice.

DO IT   Distribute and have students complete the "Don't Push My Buttons!" activity sheet. Students review and answer the questions in small groups.

TALK ABOUT IT   Students share information from their completed activity sheets. As a group, brainstorm a list of things the class can do to respect each other and avoid pushing anger buttons. Ask students: How can you let others know you are upset without blowing up?

WRITE ABOUT IT   In their journals, students respond to the prompt: What can I do when someone pushes my buttons?

Attitude Makes a Difference

LEARNING OBJECTIVE

Students will:

- learn how paying attention to their own attitude can help them deal with challenges in positive ways

MATERIALS NEEDED

The book *Making Every Day Count* by Pamela Espeland and Elizabeth Verdick, "Attitude Makes a Difference" activity sheet (page 51), and pencils or pens

LESSON PLAN

CHECK IT Brainstorm a list of stressful real-life situations students have to deal with regularly. Ask students to define the term attitude and explain the difference between positive and negative attitudes.

READ IT *Making Every Day Count*, "February 28" (page 59) and "November 2" (page 307).

DO IT Distribute and have students complete the "Attitude Makes a Difference" activity sheet. Students respond to various situations by providing positive and negative options.

TALK ABOUT IT Students share information from completed activity sheets and discuss positive and negative ways to deal with daily situations. Ask students: Who is in control of your attitude? How can starting your day with a positive attitude change the outcome of what happens? Talk about ways to start the day with a positive, rather than negative, attitude.

WRITE ABOUT IT In their journals, students respond to the prompt: Being aware of my attitude and working to keep it positive is important because...

The Anger Meter

LEARNING OBJECTIVES

Students will:

- identify different degrees of anger
- discover they have the power to choose how they respond to situations that make them angry

MATERIALS NEEDED

The book *Making Every Day Count* by Pamela Espeland and Elizabeth Verdick, "The Anger Meter" activity sheet (page 52), and pencils or pens

LESSON PLAN

CHECK IT Ask students if they all respond to situations in the same way. Tell students that one student might only feel frustrated when someone cuts in line, while another might feel very angry. Or one student might be able to ignore negative comments from others, but another might feel furious. Discuss how to recognize levels of anger students may experience in different situations. Ask students: What are the choices you can make and the actions you can take? Encourage students to consider what they learned with Stop, Think, Choose.

READ IT *Making Every Day Count*, "March 6" (page 66) and "April 20" (page 111).

DO IT Distribute and complete "The Anger Meter" activity sheet. Students read various situations and rank their anger level from 1 to 5.

TALK ABOUT IT Students share completed activity sheets. Point out similarities and differences in how they feel and react to different situations. Explain that by recognizing that others respond differently and by choosing to respect each other, students may be able to avoid some conflicts.

WRITE ABOUT IT In their journals, students respond to the prompt: Describe something that upsets you. What can you do to change how you react to it?

MORE COOL READS *Don't Sweat the Small Stuff for Teens* by Richard Carlson, "Tame Your Anger" (page 214).

I-Messages

LEARNING OBJECTIVES

Students will:

- learn to use I-messages to help them express how they feel in a positive way during conflicts
- practice using I-messages to deal with bullying situations

MATERIALS NEEDED

The book *Too Old for This, Too Young for That!* by Harriet S. Mosatche and Karen Unger, "I-Messages..." activity sheet (page 53), and pencils or pens

LESSON PLAN

CHECK IT

Introduce I-messages and discuss how sometimes people hurt our feelings intentionally, but sometimes they do it without knowing. Explain to students that using I-messages is a respectful way to let someone know how you feel and what is needed to make things right. Review the I-messages steps. The students state how they feel when something happens and what they need to make it right (I feel _____ when _____. I need _____.) Model using I-messages as often as possible, so it becomes part of the students' vocabulary.

READ IT
Too Old for This, Too Young for That!, "Being a Good Friend" (pages 101–102) and "I-messages" (page 74).

DO IT Students make a list of situations where a conflict might escalate because of a bad choice of words, actions, or tone of voice. Based on those examples, use role play to give students the opportunity to practice I-messages to solve each problem. Discuss why using I-messages to express feelings is more effective than beginning a discussion or an argument with the word "you." During this activity, students complete the "I-Messages..." sheet with phrases generated by the role playing.

TALK ABOUT IT Explain to students that it will take some time to remember to use I-messages but they will get better at it with practice. Discuss situations when the other person might not respond to I-messages in a positive way, and review options of how to respond *(walk away, ask for help, take time to cool off and think, etc.)*. Students keep their activity sheet. Refer to it during teachable moments.

WRITE ABOUT IT In their journals, students respond to the prompt: Do you think using I-messages is an effective way to solve problems? Why or why not?

Not Fair!

LEARNING OBJECTIVES
Students will:

- learn about fairness and justice
- apply the concept of being fair in their lives

MATERIALS NEEDED
The book *The Cow of No Color* by Nina Jaffe and Steve Zeitlin, "Not Fair!" activity sheet (page 54), and pencils or pens

LESSON PLAN

CHECK IT Students define *fairness* and *justice*. Discuss how fairness and justice relate to the golden rule. Often people are judged unfairly because we don't take the time to get to know them. Ask students: Have you ever felt pressured by your friends to treat someone unfairly even though you didn't agree?

READ IT *The Cow of No Color*, "The Cow of No Color" (pages 10–13) or "The Sound of Work" (pages 14–17) are both multicultural tales of poetic justice.

DO IT Distribute and have students complete the "Not Fair!" activity sheet. As a follow-up activity, ask students to develop a list of the things they can do to promote fairness *(avoid gossip, stand up for others, play by the rules, agree*

to disagree, be inclusive, accept differences, give everyone a chance, etc.).*

TALK ABOUT IT Students review information from the completed activity and choose the best ideas from each group to create a "Top 10 Ways to Be Fair" poster for the classroom.

WRITE ABOUT IT In their journals, students respond to the prompt: Describe a situation when you felt someone was treated unfairly. How did you feel about it and what did you do?

Perfectly Imperfect

LEARNING OBJECTIVES
Students will:

- learn to accept their unique gifts and talents
- discuss the meaning of *perfection*

MATERIALS NEEDED
The book *Making Every Day Count* by Pamela Espeland and Elizabeth Verdick, "Perfectly Imperfect" activity sheet (page 55), and pencils or pens

LESSON PLAN

CHECK IT Discuss with students what it means to be perfect. Ask students: Do you think being perfect is important? How realistic is that? If the opposite of perfect is imperfect, how do we all deal with that?

READ IT *Making Every Day Count*, "April 21" (page 112) and "April 22" (page 113).

DO IT Distribute and have students complete the "Perfectly Imperfect" activity sheet.

TALK ABOUT IT Tell students that part of growing up is taking risks, learning from our mistakes, asking questions, and practicing skills so we can get better at what we do. Ask students: Who decides what *perfect* means? What are the consequences of always expecting perfection? Have students think of imperfections that make people unique.

WRITE ABOUT IT In their journals, students respond to the prompt: Do you expect yourself to be perfect? Do you think other people expect you to be perfect? How do you feel about that and what can you do about it?

Discovering Our Feelings Quiz

To assess student progress, use the quiz on page 56. *(Answers: 1-F, 2-F, 3-F, 4-T, 5-F, 6-a, 7-d, 8-d, 9-feelings, important, 10-predict, mistake)*

Safe & Caring Vocabulary

Fill in the blanks below with the correct words from the list:

discovering	feelings	experience	emotions
right	uncomfortable	powerful	healthy
positive	choose	understand	journey
recognize	important	communicate	choices
people	understanding	stressed	aware

It is _____ to be _____ of the _____

we _____ and what we _____ to do with

them. _____ our feelings is a significant

_____, because the more we learn to _____

how we feel, the more we _____ ourselves. Some

_____ are _____ and others can make us

_____ and _____. Recognizing

stress and knowing how to make the _____ _____

is a _____, _____ step toward

_____ how to _____ with

_____ around us in a positive way.

Define the word **stress**. _____

_____

_____

_____

we are
a safe
& caring
school.

From Safe & Caring Schools® Grades 6–8 by Katia S. Petersen, Ph.D., copyright © 2008. Free Spirit Publishing Inc., Minneapolis, MN; www.freespirit.com. This page may be photocopied for individual, classroom, or small group work only. For other uses, call 800-735-7323.

OCTOBER

Safe & Caring WORD FIND

Find and circle the words listed at the bottom of the page.

(Hint: Answers can run forward, backward, up, down, or diagonally.)

B	E	S	L	U	P	M	I	V	C	C	E	O
P	R	O	U	N	E	S	U	F	N	D	M	L
L	E	V	E	D	A	H	L	D	U	O	O	O
P	M	E	N	E	S	Y	P	T	Q	L	T	R
M	B	R	A	R	N	E	I	H	U	R	I	T
S	A	W	R	S	P	T	T	I	E	L	O	N
S	R	H	E	T	T	H	F	N	Z	D	N	O
E	R	E	C	A	I	R	G	K	V	O	U	C
N	A	L	O	N	E	L	Y	N	I	Q	N	O
E	S	M	G	D	A	F	H	T	O	V	O	A
R	S	E	N	I	P	V	C	Z	L	D	I	F
A	E	D	I	N	H	A	Q	F	E	N	T	E
W	D	G	Z	G	E	N	F	S	N	S	C	E
A	N	G	E	R	U	D	S	H	T	I	E	L
A	L	F	T	N	B	E	Z	V	L	G	F	I
M	L	A	C	U	R	H	A	L	O	N	R	N
U	A	Q	E	T	Q	V	Y	U	N	A	E	G
F	R	U	S	T	R	A	T	E	D	L	P	S

CALM	THINK	IMPULSE	EMOTION
UNDERSTANDING	ATTITUDE	OVERWHELMED	PERFECTION
SIGNAL	EMBARRASSED	RECOGNIZE	REACTION
ANGER	CONTROL	STRESSED	FEELINGS
AWARENESS	LONELY	FRUSTRATED	VIOLENT

we are
a safe
& caring
school.

UN-MIX IT!

Sometimes the lyrics of life need to get straightened out.

1. surprised
2. confident
3. lonely
4. hopeless
5. concerned
6. jealous
7. worried
8. annoyed
9. important
10. impatient
11. energized
12. bored

Un-mix the 12 feelings words listed. Write the numbers of the un-mixed words in the circles below.

Choose one of the feelings. Write about a situation when this feeling was all mixed up. What did you do?

_____
_____
_____
_____
_____
_____
_____
_____
_____
_____

○ shoelpse
○ rednncoce
○ zegredien
○ drebo
○ tantiepim
○ eynoll
○ reidorw
○ yendnao
○ sualoej
○ nodfenitc
○ ramiontpt
○ rsusperid

we aRe a SaFe & CaRiNG SCHOOL.

IT'S ... all ... connected

Our thoughts, feelings, attitudes, and actions can affect each other.

Situation	Your Thoughts	Emoticon	Your Feelings	Your Attitude	Your Actions
You were not asked to go to the movies with your friends.	Maybe they don't like me.	😐	I feel hurt and sad.	Who cares about them!	I'll just ignore them.
You tried hard but you didn't do as well on a test as you'd hoped to.					
You're blamed for something you didn't do.					
Someone spreads rumors about you.					
You're in a school play and forget your lines.					

Emoticon Library

🙂 🙁 😮 😐 😕 😟 😳 😠 😢 😲

We ARE
a SAFE
& CARING
SCHOOL.

can you PREDICT?

Friend Situation

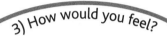

1) You and a friend agree to meet for a movie that you've been waiting to see. At the last moment your friend calls and can't make it.

2) PREDICT what you think you might do.

_____
_____
_____
_____
_____

3) How would you feel?
_____
_____
_____
_____
_____

Family Situation

1) Your little brother goes into your room without permission and plays with the model you made for class.

2) PREDICT what you think you might do.

_____
_____
_____
_____
_____

3) How would you feel?
_____
_____
_____
_____
_____

School Situation

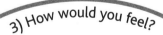

1) You try out for a particular role in the school play, but you are picked for a different one.

2) PREDICT what you think you might do.

_____
_____
_____
_____
_____

3) How would you feel?
_____
_____
_____
_____
_____

Neighborhood Situation

1) A new family moves in next door and they have a son that hangs out with a group of troublemakers at school.

2) PREDICT what you think you might do.

_____
_____
_____
_____
_____

3) How would you feel?
_____
_____
_____
_____
_____

we are a safe & caring school.

WHAT HAPPENS WHEN I GET ANGRY?

1. Angry

- My hands turn into fists
- My hands feel cold
- My eyes hurt
- My face feels hot
- My head aches
- My stomach hurts
- My heart races
- My muscles get tight
- _____
- _____

2. Better

read

listen to music

talk to a friend

have quiet time

draw or write in a journal

count to 10 until calm

exercise

add your own

add your own

take a walk

3. Calm

talk to a grown-up

breathe slowly

WE ARE A SAFE & CARING SCHOOL.

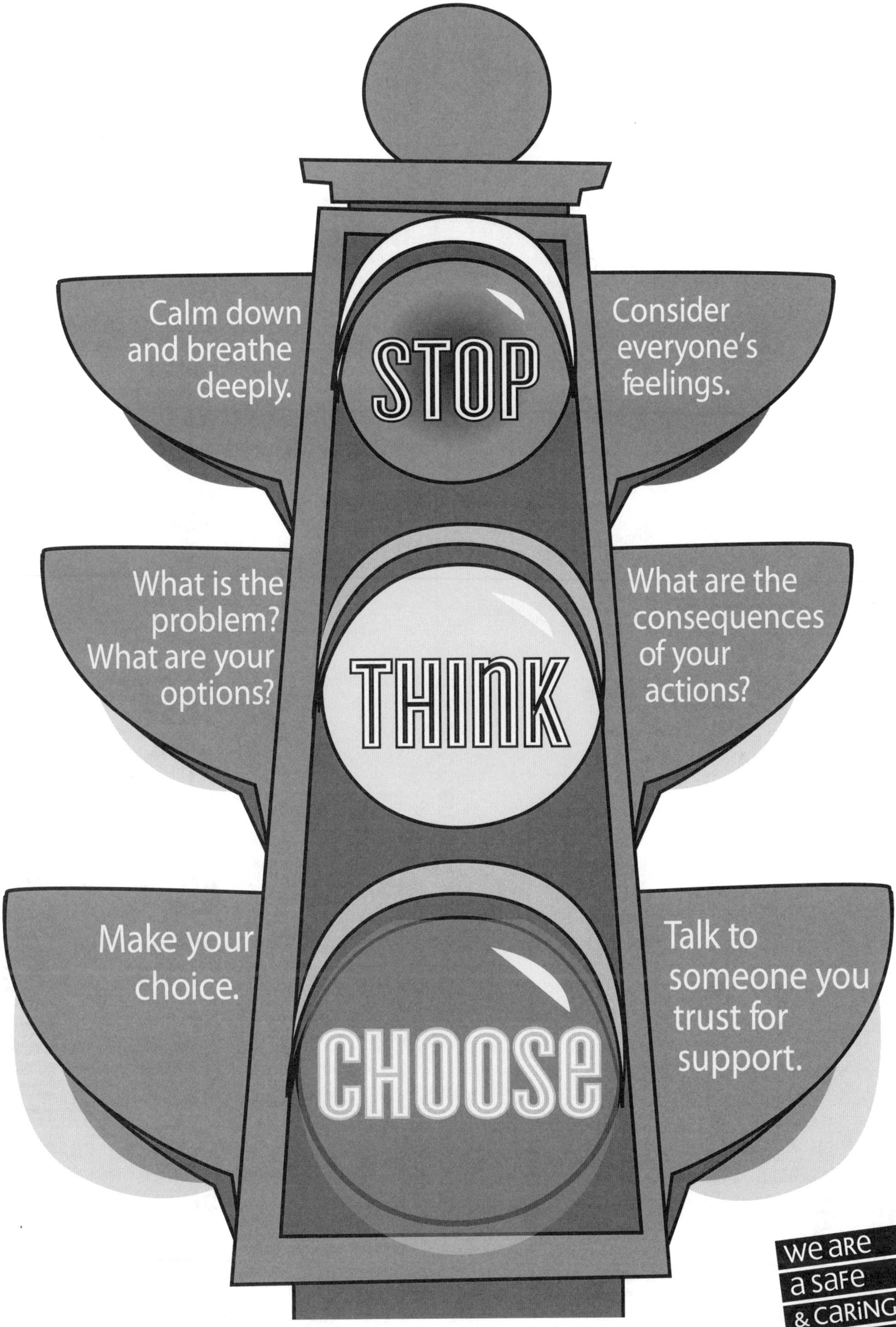

Calm down and breathe deeply.

Consider everyone's feelings.

STOP

What is the problem? What are your options?

What are the consequences of your actions?

THINK

Make your choice.

Talk to someone you trust for support.

CHOOSE

we are a safe & caring school.

DON'T PUSH MY BUTTONS!

Hey, everyone gets angry!

 Bothered

 Annoyed

 Ticked Off

 Angry

 Really Mad!

Is it ever okay to get angry? Why?

What kinds of things make me angry?

How often do I get angry?

What happens to my body when I get angry?

When I feel angry, I usually...

WE ARE a SAFE & CARING SCHOOL.

ATTITUDE MAKES A DIFFERENCE

We all have challenges...

...it's how we handle them that counts.

Situation	Describe a positive way you can deal with it.	Describe a negative way to handle it.
1) Someone dares you to do something you know is wrong.		
2) A friend you trusted is gossiping about you online.		
3) You wake up grumpy and want to scream when your mother tells you you'll be late for school.		
4) You got home very late even though your parents asked you to respect your curfew.		
5) You have ONE extra ticket to a game and you know your two best friends would love to go with you.		

we are
a safe
& caring
school.

Write a number from 1 to 5 in the Anger Meters to describe how you might feel in the following situations. Then, write what you would do in response.

Someone pressures you to do something you don't want to do. How would you feel and what would you do? _____

_____

You shared something personal with a friend and asked her to keep it private but she didn't. How would you feel and what would you do? _____

_____

A group of kids are telling racist jokes during recess. How would you feel and what would you do? _____

_____

A classmate borrows a pen from you during a test, but you ended up being blamed for talking and cheating. How would you feel and what would you do? _____

_____

_____

Your friends told you they will be out of town and cannot get together this weekend, then you run into them at the movies. How would you feel and what would you do?

_____

_____

You're always there for your friend, but when you need support, he or she never gives you the time. How would you feel and what would you do? _____

_____

Write a situation of your own and tell how you would feel and what you would do: _____

_____

we aRe
a SaFe
& CaRiNG
SCHOOL.

I-MESSAGES...

When you're in a tough spot, use I-messages to help figure out a solution. Follow these steps...

1) I feel...(write how you feel)

_____

_____

_____

_____

_____

_____

2) When...(write what happened)

_____

_____

_____

_____

_____

_____

_____

3) I need...(write what you need to find a solution)

_____

_____

_____

_____

_____

_____

we are a safe & caring SCHOOL.

NOT FaIR!

Have you ever been treated unfairly? What did you do?

Have you ever treated someone else unfairly? What happened?

How do you feel when you're treated unfairly?

Have you seen a friend treated unfairly? What did you do?

Action!

we aRe
a SaFe
& CaRiNG
SCHOOL.

PERFECTLY IMPERFECT

Define **perfect.**

_____
_____
_____
_____

Do you expect yourself to be perfect?

On a scale of 1–10 how perfect do you think a person must be to be accepted by others?

(Fill in the bar chart below up to the number of your answer)

0   1   2   3   4   5   6   7   8   9   10

not perfect   perfect

What does **perfect** look, feel, and sound like?

_____
_____
_____
_____
_____

Can anybody really be PERFECT?

Yes ☐ No ☐ Why? _____
_____
_____
_____
_____

we are
a safe
& caring
SCHOOL.

DISCOVERING OUR FEELINGS QUIZ

True or False (circle the correct answer)

1) Others can't possibly know how I feel. . . . . **True / False**

2) If we're always careful about how everyone is feeling, we'll never get anything done. . . . . **True / False**

3) It helps to pretend or just hide our feelings when we're angry or having a bad day. . . . . **True / False**

4) When we are in touch with our feelings, it helps us understand the feelings of others. . . . . **True / False**

5) The best thing to do is never show others how you are feeling. . . . . **True / False**

Multiple Choice (circle the correct answer)

6) When you are angry:
   a. it is good to Stop, Think, Choose.
   b. you can't help it when you take it out on others.
   c. nobody can help.
   d. all of the above

7) Stop, Think, Choose helps us:
   a. find the best solution to a problem.
   b. calm down when we are upset.
   c. think about our options.
   d. all of the above

8) To understand how others feel:
   a. think about how you would feel in the same situation.
   b. ask them.
   c. listen to their voice and watch how they're acting.
   d. all of the above

Fill in the Blanks

9) Our thoughts and our f_____ are both i_____.

10) Try to p_____ how you will feel before doing something that may be a m_____ .

Real-Life Writing

Have you ever been torn between one feeling and another? What can you do when your feelings get mixed up?

we aRe
a SaFe
& CaRiNG
SCHOOL.

NOVEMBER
My Support System

- Creating a Support System
- Asking for Help

- Friendship
- Appreciation

Monthly Objectives

Students will:

- discuss the qualities of friendship and how good friends can be an important part of their support system
- learn the importance of having a support system and how to ask for help from people they know and trust

Social Emotional Definitions

Appreciation: A feeling or expression of gratitude. A positive opinion and recognition of someone's qualities.

Courage: The strength to act according to your beliefs and do the right thing.

Criticize: To point out the faults of others, or to find something wrong or bad about them.

Curiosity: The desire to learn about new ideas, places, and people.

Dependable: Able to be trusted and counted on to do something.

Discovery: The process of finding out about something for the first time.

Friendship: Forming a bond with someone who is accepting and supportive of you in positive ways.

Gratitude: A feeling of being thankful to someone for helping you out.

Loyalty: The quality of being true and committed to someone or something.

Stress: A condition of mental, emotional, and/or physical strain.

Support: To give someone help and encouragement.

Trustworthy: Able to be depended upon.

TEACHING TIPS

- As a teacher, look for opportunities to model desirable behaviors.
- Use teachable moments to reinforce monthly themes.
- Integrate the teaching of social and emotional skills into your daily routine.

NOVEMBER INTEGRATED ACTIVITIES

In addition to the specific lesson plans for this month, you can use these optional ideas to integrate and extend the Safe & Caring themes into your daily routines and across the curricular areas.

LANGUAGE ARTS

- Have students write an article for the school newspaper about teens and stress. Give tips and ideas on how to deal with stress in positive ways.
- Encourage students to write public service announcements or commercials about friendship. Present them during morning news or daily announcements.
- Have students list the qualities of good friends and create miniposters showing how to build positive friendships.
- Create a "Friendship Instruction Book." Fill it with students' ideas on how to make and keep friends.

LITERATURE

- Students read books on friendship like *The Friendship* by Mildred D. Taylor. Discuss the qualities of friendship between the characters.
- Students write and act out a story about the true meaning of friendship.
- Students read books where characters learn to ask for help from people they know and trust.

SOCIAL STUDIES

- Students create a map of the support system that exists within their school community, complete with names of people that students can rely on for help.
- Students create a timeline showing past and present modes of communication used in society. Compare the two as a class. Discuss common communication methods used today, especially by young people.

ART

- Students create posters describing the qualities of friendship. Use old magazines to cut out pictures or have students create their own.
- Students create a friendship collage or mural. Have students take turns working it until it is a finished "masterpiece."
- Students read *Vincent van Gogh: Portrait of an Artist* by Jan Greenberg and Sandra Jordan. Using Vincent's style, have students paint a self-portrait or a portrait of a friend.

MUSIC

- Students research songs about friendship both for listening and singing. Try "You've Got a Friend in Me" by Randy Newman and Lyle Lovett or "I'll Be There for You" (theme song from the TV show *Friends*) by The Rembrandts.

MATH

- Students take a survey to find out which forms of communication are most commonly used among people in school. Students compare students and adults and complete a Venn diagram.
- Students create a graph that shows what students consider to be the most important friendship skills in 6th, 7th, and 8th grades.

SCIENCE

- Study about the physiological reactions people have when experiencing stress. Compare how adults and young people might react to stress, and discuss healthy ways to deal with it.

Safe & Caring Vocabulary and Word Find

LEARNING OBJECTIVES

Students will:

- be introduced to the vocabulary that supports learning how to be a safe and caring classroom
- internalize the vocabulary as they use it throughout the month and year in real-life situations

MATERIALS NEEDED

"Safe & Caring Vocabulary" (page 64) and "Safe & Caring Word Find" (page 65) activity sheets, pencils, and dictionaries

LESSON PLAN

Use the vocabulary activities to introduce the concepts and common language associated with this month's theme. Throughout the month, use the words in writing, spelling, storytelling, and dealing with conflict situations.

For "Safe & Caring Vocabulary," students unscramble the words to fill in the blanks. (A safe and *caring* school is a *supportive* place where everyone deserves to feel *respected*. That means people are *understanding* and *dependable*. It is everyone's *responsibility* to *give* support to others. Having *trustworthy* friends we can *count* on when we need *help* keeps us from getting *stuck* in a bad *situation*. To have a strong *support* system, we must also learn to *give* help to others.)

For "Safe & Caring Word Find," discuss what the words mean after completing the page. You may want students to work in pairs to help each other.

For an added challenge, at the end of each month, have students work individually or in small groups to create their own word find puzzles, using the words defined in "Social Emotional Definitions" (see page 57).

My Support System

LEARNING OBJECTIVES

Students will:

- learn to identify their personal support systems
- learn how to get support when they need it

MATERIALS NEEDED

The book *People Who Care About You* by Pamela Espeland and Elizabeth Verdick, "My Support System" activity sheet (page 66), and pencils or pens

LESSON PLAN

CHECK IT Introduce the topic by describing the support beams on a bridge and explaining their importance. Ask students: What would happen if bridges did not have strong support beams? Can you relate that thought to your own lives. Everyone, including adults, needs support. Ask students: What kinds of support do you need and who gives it to you?

READ IT In *People Who Care About You*, "Caring School Climate" (pages 56–65), kids learn how to build one of the six Support Assets: Caring School Climate.

DO IT Distribute and have students complete the "My Support System" activity sheet. Students list the people in their support system and how these people support them.

TALK ABOUT IT Review with students where they can go for help in their school community. Discuss appropriate ways to ask for help and explain the importance of confidentiality. Let the students know that sometimes it will take a while before they find the right person to give the support they need. Encourage them to keep asking and not to give up.

WRITE ABOUT IT In their journals, students respond to the prompt: Think of a time you needed help making a decision or dealing with a tough situation. Did you have people to support you? Who were they and how did they help?

MORE COOL READS *Just as Long as We're Together* by Judy Blume. Recommended for girls, this first-person narrative touches on many themes found in Blume's previous novels: friendship, emerging sexuality, body weight, family, and menstruation.

Do You Understand Me Now?

LEARNING OBJECTIVES

Students will:

- learn how to utilize their personal support systems
- learn how to communicate their feelings and needs to others

MATERIALS NEEDED

The book *Making Every Day Count* by Pamela Espeland and Elizabeth Verdick, "Do You Understand Me Now?" activity sheet (page 67), and pencils or pens

LESSON PLAN

CHECK IT   Ask students: Do you ever feel like other people do not understand you? Why do you suppose this is? Discuss how effective communication can reduce misunderstandings and conflicts.

READ IT   *Making Every Day Count*, "January 21" (page 21) and "July 29" (page 211) .

DO IT   Distribute and have students complete the "Do You Understand Me Now?" activity sheet. Students choose one member from each group along the path they feel comfortable going to for help. Then they explain why they chose each person.

TALK ABOUT IT   Review information from the completed activity and discuss how students chose where to go for support and why. Ask students: How do you show support for people around you? Take it a step further by introducing and discussing the differences between effective and ineffective communication.

WRITE ABOUT IT   In their journals, students respond to the prompt: Describe a time you had a misunderstanding with a friend or a family member. Were you communicating effectively with each other?

MORE COOL READS   In *The Moves Make the Man* by Bruce Brooks, two boys form an unlikely friendship.

Stressing the Positive

LEARNING OBJECTIVES

Students will:

- learn that stress is a normal part of life
- review positive and negative ways to respond to stress

MATERIALS NEEDED

The book *Too Stressed to Think?* by Annie Fox and Ruth Kirschner, "Stressing the Positive" activity sheet (page 68), and pencils or pens

LESSON PLAN

CHECK IT   Define stress and discuss how stress impacts our lives. Have students brainstorm the things that create stress for them. Ask students: What are your choices for dealing with things that stress you?

READ IT   *Too Stressed to Think?*, "Stress 101" (pages 7–17).

DO IT   Distribute and have students complete the "Stressing the Positive" activity sheet. Students rate situations as to how stressful they are and then analyze two specific stressors.

TALK ABOUT IT   Discuss students' answers on the activity sheet. Encourage students to ask for support when they need it. Remind them they do not have to solve all their problems alone.

WRITE ABOUT IT   In their journals, students respond to the prompt: Describe a time when stress affected your schoolwork and your ability to make good choices.

MORE COOL READS   *Fighting Invisible Tigers* by Earl Hipp discusses the pressures and problems encountered by teenagers and provides information on life skills, stress management, assertiveness, positive self-talk, and more.

Stress Stoppers

LEARNING OBJECTIVES

Students will:

- learn healthy ways to lower their stress level
- identify the things that create stress in their lives

MATERIALS NEEDED

The book *Stress Can Really Get on Your Nerves!* by Trevor Romain and Elizabeth Verdick, "Stress Stoppers" activity sheet (page 69), and pencils or pens

LESSON PLAN

CHECK IT   Ask students: How many of you have experienced stress? Explain that stress is a normal part of life and that learning how to respond to stress in positive ways takes practice.

READ IT   *Stress Can Really Get on Your Nerves!* uses silly jokes and lighthearted cartoons along with serious advice to help readers recognize the causes of stress and its effects and learn how to handle worry, anxiety, and stress.

DO IT With the "Stress Stoppers" activity sheet, students identify stressful situations and what they can do to lower their stress level.

TALK ABOUT IT Review completed activity sheets. Help students make the connection between personal choices and stress. Ask students: What things do you have control over and what things can't you control?

WRITE ABOUT IT In their journals, students respond to the prompt: Have you ever felt so stressed that your emotions took over and you felt physically ill? What did you do?

MORE COOL READS *The Chalk Box Kid* by Clyde Robert Bulla. When Gregory experiences several upsets in his life, he responds by creating a chalk garden on the charred walls of a burned-out factory. Gregory finds a voice through his art and is finally able to find his own place in the world.

Who Is a True Friend?

LEARNING OBJECTIVES

Students will:

- learn how to identify the qualities of a good friend
- practice getting along in small groups

MATERIALS NEEDED

The book *More If You Had to Choose, What Would You Do?* by Sandra McLeod Humphrey, "Who Is a True Friend?" activity sheet (page 70) or a transparency, writing and drawing utensils, and posterboard

LESSON PLAN

CHECK IT As a class, make a list of the characteristics of a good friend. Ask students: Is it easy to make friends you can really trust and count on?

READ IT *More If You Had to Choose, What Would You Do?*, "Not Exactly" (pages 15–18).

DO IT Distribute and have students complete the "Who Is a True Friend?" activity sheet and discuss answers in the large group. Another option is to make an overhead transparency of the worksheet and complete it as a class. Then, divide the class into four or five small groups. Ask each group to create a poster using one of the following ideas:

- How can I be a good friend?
- How do I know I can trust my friends?
- How do I show support to my friends?
- How do I make new friends?

TALK ABOUT IT Each group presents its poster to the class. The posters can be displayed in the hallway or in the classroom.

WRITE ABOUT IT In their journals, students respond to the prompt: Having a friend I can depend on is important to me because...

Finding Your Friendship Factors

LEARNING OBJECTIVES

Students will:

- review their key friend requirements
- identify the true meaning of friendship

MATERIALS NEEDED

The book *More If You Had to Choose, What Would You Do?* by Sandra McLeod Humphrey, "Finding Your Friendship Factors" activity sheet (page 71), and pencils or pens

LESSON PLAN

CHECK IT Discuss qualities that are important in a friend. Ask students: Why would someone hurt their friends while trying to gain popularity? Do true friends try to get each other into trouble by pressuring them to make bad choices?

READ IT *More If You Had to Choose, What Would You Do?*, "Instant Replay" (pages 33–36).

DO IT Distribute and have students complete the "Finding Your Friendship Factors" activity sheet.

TALK ABOUT IT Have students share their friendship factors and stories about true friendship. Discuss with students how sometimes friends hurt each other because they want to be popular with others. Discuss how friends should support and inspire each other. Emphasize that loyalty and honesty in a friendship are more important than popularity.

WRITE ABOUT IT In their journals, students respond to the prompt: How important is being popular and what are you willing to do to be popular?

MORE COOL READS In *Water Sky* by Jean Craighead George, Lincoln must choose between his Ologok ancestry and his belief in saving whales from extinction.

Appreciate It!

LEARNING OBJECTIVES

Students will:

- learn the meaning and importance of appreciation
- apply the golden rule to the concept of appreciation for others

MATERIALS NEEDED

The book *Character Building Day by Day* by Anne D. Mather and Louise B. Weldon, "Appreciate It!" activity sheet (page 72), and pencils or pens

LESSON PLAN

CHECK IT Define the word *appreciation*. Discuss the difference between the two dictionary definitions: (1) a feeling or expression of gratitude and (2) a favorable opinion of something. Ask students: Is it possible to feel both these aspects of appreciation for a friend?

READ IT *Character Building Day by Day*, "Someone to Talk With" (page 113).

DO IT Distribute and have students complete the "Appreciate It!" activity sheet.

TALK ABOUT IT Students share why they think appreciation is important and give examples of how people show appreciation. Make a list of how class members can show appreciation for one another.

WRITE ABOUT IT In their journals, students respond to the prompt: Do you feel appreciated by your family and friends? Why or why not?

Help Department

LEARNING OBJECTIVE

Students will:

- explore who to call when they or someone they know needs help

MATERIALS NEEDED

The book *Too Stressed to Think?* by Annie Fox and Ruth Kirschner, "Help Department" activity sheet (page 73), and pencils or pens

LESSON PLAN

CHECK IT There are people and services in their community where students can get the support they need. Ask students: Do you know where you can go for support?

READ IT *Too Stressed to Think?*, "Get the Help You Need" (pages 142–148).

DO IT Have students complete the "Help Department" activity sheet.

TALK ABOUT IT Tell students that just as there are repair people you can ask to fix things that are broken, there are people you can ask for help when you or a situation you're in needs fixing. Review activity sheets and discuss the importance of reaching out for support.

WRITE ABOUT IT In their journals, students respond to the prompt: The person I usually talk to when I feel worried, upset, or stressed is _____ because...

Peer Pressure

LEARNING OBJECTIVES

Students will:

- learn how peer pressure affects their lives in positive and negative ways
- learn specific methods they can use to deal with peer pressure

MATERIALS NEEDED

The book *The Courage to Be Yourself*, edited by Al Desetta, "Peer Pressure" activity sheet (page 74), writing and drawing utensils, and posterboard

LESSON PLAN

CHECK IT Students define *peer pressure*. Ask students: When have you experienced positive or negative peer pressure? Help them make the connection between supportive friends who influence them in positive ways and others who influence them in negative ways.

READ IT *The Courage to Be Yourself*, "Losing My Friends to Weed" (pages 39–42).

DO IT Students work in small groups to complete the "Peer Pressure" activity sheet, which shows kids trying to negatively influence their peers. The group then creates a poster showing a positive peer pressure situation.

TALK ABOUT IT A spokesperson from each small group shares the group's completed activity sheet and poster. Discuss ways students can deal with both negative and positive peer pressure. What are the consequences when kids give in to negative peer pressure? What can you do to resist negative peer pressure? What can you do or say to influence your peers in a *positive* way?

WRITE ABOUT IT In their journals, students respond to the prompt: Tell about a time you felt pressured to do something you did not want to do. What happened? Why did you react the way you did?

So-Called Friends

LEARNING OBJECTIVES

Students will:

- discuss the pressure to fit in with others
- learn how to stay true to themselves by standing up for what they believe in

MATERIALS NEEDED

The book *Character Building Day by Day* by Anne D. Mather and Louise B. Weldon, "So-Called Friends" activity sheet (page 75), pencils or pens, and index cards

LESSON PLAN

CHECK IT Ask students: Have you ever known someone you thought was a friend, but who ended up creating problems and getting you in trouble? Why might someone behave that way? Why do people succumb to negative pressure from others?

READ IT *Character Building Day by Day*, "The Tree and the Pond" (page 75).

DO IT Divide students into small groups. On index cards, students write scenarios involving kids being pressured to do something that will get them into trouble. Collect the cards, shuffle them, and redistribute them among the groups. Each group resolves the situation it receives.

TALK ABOUT IT Using the scenarios and the solutions, the groups role-play how to stand up to negative peer pressure. Have the class critique the solutions. Ask students: Do you think the solutions will work? Why or why not?

WRITE ABOUT IT In their journals, students respond to the prompt: Why is it hard for kids to deal with negative peer pressure?

MORE COOL READS *The Courage to Be Yourself*, edited by Al Desetta, "Which Crowd Did You Pick?" (pages 29–30).

My Support System Quiz

To assess student progress, use the quiz on page 76. *(Answers: 1-F, 2-F, 3-T, 4-T, 5-T, 6-d, 7-d, 8-b, 9-communication, receiving, 10-pressure, negative)*

Safe & Caring Vocabulary

Unscramble the words to complete the sentences.

A safe and _ _ _ _ _ _ school is a _ _ _ _ _ _ _ _ _ _
graicn   tpseruvpio

place where everyone deserves to feel _ _ _ _ _ _ _ _ _.
drepstece

That means people are _ _ _ _ _ _ _ _ _ _ _ _ and
nuieganrdntsd

_ _ _ _ _ _ _ _ _ _. It is everyone's _ _ _ _ _ _ _ _ _ _ _ _ _
needdlpeba   spseryitinloib

to _ _ _ _ support to others. Having _ _ _ _ _ _ _ _ _ _ _
vegi   yhotrtwutrs

friends we can _ _ _ _ _ on when we need _ _ _ _ keeps
otcnu   phel

us from getting _ _ _ _ _ in a bad _ _ _ _ _ _ _ _ _. To
custk   inostiuta

have a strong _ _ _ _ _ _ _ system, we must also learn
torpusp

to _ _ _ _ help to others.
iegv

Define the word **supportive**. _____

_____

_____

Write a sentence using the words **responsibility** and **trust**.

_____

_____

_____

we are
a safe
& caring
school.

SAFE & CARING WORD FIND

Find and circle the words listed at the bottom of the page.

(Hint: Answers can run forward, backward, up, down, or diagonally.)

B	P	U	G	R	A	T	I	T	U	D	E	O		O
E	G	A	R	U	O	C	N	E	B	C	S			E
L	N	R	A	B	S	O	L	V	E	K	U			C
P	A	P	P	R	E	C	I	A	T	I	O			N
H	E	L	P	R	F	U	L	C	S	F	Q	R		A
R	P	C	R	Q	C	E	R	F	Y	S	E	N		T
E	I	K	E	Z	K	M	S	K	Z	R	N			S
S	H	G	C	R	I	T	S	C	I	Z	M	G		S
P	S	Y	I	A	D	V	O	C	A	T	E	D		S
O	N	K	T	C	E	N	Z	C	S	Y	L	I		A
N	O	I	U	I	R	C	I	G	C	Y	B	S		U
S	I	T	O	L	B	E	T	E	L	Z	O	C		T
I	T	U	N	K	Z	U	P	P	Z	R	O	R		R
B	A	T	S	U	P	P	O	R	T	T	Q	P	V	E
L	L	N	D	E	P	E	N	D	A	B	L	E		L
E	E	D	E	P	E	N	D	S	H	I	P	C	R	A
F	R	I	E	N	D	S	H	I	P	C	R	A		
U	T	R	U	S	T	W	O	R	T	H	Y	X		

CRITICIZE	ADVOCATE	HELPFUL	SUPPORT
TRUSTWORTHY	RELAX	ASSISTANCE	ACCEPT
GENEROUS	PROBLEM	APPRECIATION	GRATITUDE
DEPENDABLE	SOLVE	STUCK	FRIENDSHIP
RESPONSIBLE	RELATIONSHIP	DISCOVERY	ENCOURAGE

we are
a safe
& caring
SCHOOL.

NOVEMBER

Neighborhood

My Support System

Why is it important to have people who can support us?

School

Family

Name two family members who support you.

Explain one way your family supports you.

Friends

Name two friends who support you.

How do your friends support you?

School

Name two people at school you can ask for help.

What kind of support do you need at school?

we are a safe & caring SCHOOL.

DO YOU UNDERSTAND ME NOW?

What can you do to let people know how you feel and what you need?

_____
_____
_____
_____

Do you feel the people around you really know you?

Yes ☐

No ☐

Coach

Who: _____
_____

Why: _____
_____

Family Friend

Who: _____
_____

Why: _____
_____

Teacher

Who: _____
_____

Why: _____
_____

Boy/Girl Friend

Who: _____
_____

Why: _____
_____

On the *Path* of life, who understands you the most and why?

Friends

Who: _____
_____

Why: _____
_____

Counselor

Who: _____
_____

Why: _____
_____

Family

Who: _____
_____

Why: _____
_____

Other

Who: _____
_____

Why: _____
_____

Start Here

we aRe a saFe & CaRiNG SCHOOL.

STRESSING THE POSITIVE

Stress is part of life. It's how we deal with it that counts. Circle how stressful a situation can be on a scale from 1 to 4.

Choose two of your worst stressors. Write positive (+) and negative (−) ways you might handle them in the future.

Stress-O-Meter

	That's easy!	Interesting challenge	Why me?	Oh no!
doing homework	1	2	3	4
making friends	1	2	3	4
working on chores	1	2	3	4
talking to parents	1	2	3	4
the way I look	1	2	3	4
making choices	1	2	3	4
being on time	1	2	3	4
doing things right	1	2	3	4
someone is mad at me	1	2	3	4
being included	1	2	3	4
being liked	1	2	3	4
being responsible	1	2	3	4
being put on the spot	1	2	3	4
getting good grades	1	2	3	4

Why me?

1)

+ −

Oh no!

2)

+ −

we aRe a SaFe & CaRiNG SCHOOL.

Tired? Stressed-out? Crabby?

STRESS STOPPERS

are what you need when there's too much stress in your life.

What are some of the things that stress you out?

_____

_____

_____

_____

Things others can do to help me lower my stress.

My friends can be good listeners when I have a problem.

Things I can do myself to help lower my stress.

I can leave enough time to do my chores or homework so I don't have to rush.

we are a safe & caring school.

WHO IS A TRUE FRIEND?

It can be tricky sometimes but it's important to know...

A true friend is someone who...

- accepts you for who you are .... **True** or **False**
- dares you to do things that might get you in trouble .... **True** or **False**
- cares about how you feel.................................... **True** or **False**
- takes time to help... **True** or **False**
- calls only when he or she needs something.. **True** or **False**
- demands you do something you don't want to do if you want to stay friends .... **True** or **False**
- you can call if you need to talk about something.. **True** or **False**

Describe the qualities you look for in a friend.

Do you have a friend you can count on?

_____
_____
_____
_____
_____
_____
_____

Yes

No

If yes, what are a few things you like about your friend?

_____

If no, what can you do to change that to a yes?

_____
_____

We are a safe & caring school.

FINDING YOUR FRIENDSHIP FACTORS

Why is it important to be careful when you choose your friends?

_____

_____

_____

Rate these key **Friendship Factors**

1) must have   2) really want   3) don't think so   4) no way!

____ fun to be with

____ stands up for others

____ bossy

____ responsible

____ controlling

____ doesn't share

____ likes to gossip

____ intelligent

____ loud

____ trusting

____ good listener

____ teases

____ motivated

____ often sad

____ dependable

____ good athlete

____ forgetful

____ pushy

____ creative

____ likes school

____ fair

____ hilarious

____ generous

____ unkind

____ selfish

____ rough and tough

____ energetic

____ understanding

____ shy

____ likes pets

____ _____

____ _____

Using your top three Friendship Factors, write a journal entry about friendship.

_____

_____

_____

_____

we are
a safe
& caring
school.

APPRECIATE IT!

Why is it important to appreciate others?

Define **appreciation**: _____

_____

_____

Remember the golden rule?

One way to show appreciation for others is...

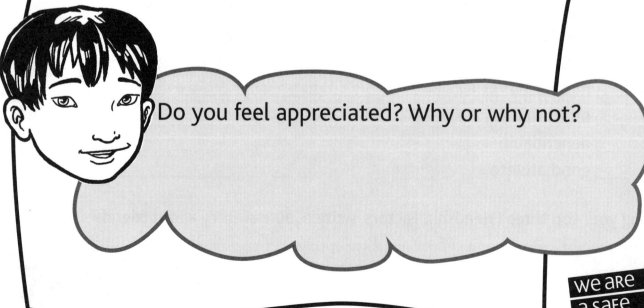

Do you feel appreciated? Why or why not?

WE ARE
A SAFE
& CARiNG
SCHOOL.

HELP DEPARTMENT

Who might you call if...

Steam is coming from your family car's radiator. _____

You saw someone shoplifting. _____

Water is leaking in your home. _____

The electricity goes off. _____

Your pet needs its shots. _____

Your computer is broken. _____

There is a fire on the stove. _____

You need help studying for a test. _____

The roof springs a leak. _____

You need braces on your teeth. _____

Your grades are failing. _____

You smell gas in your house. _____

Your bike is stolen. _____

Someone gets hurt in an accident and needs to go to the hospital. _____

Someone is being bullied. _____

You overhear someone planning to vandalize the school. _____

Someone is sending you mean emails or text messages. _____

we are a safe & caring school.

PEER PRESSURE

If you've ever felt pressure to do something you didn't want to, you've felt negative...

What would you say?

Are these positive or negative responses to peer pressure? Draw a plus ⊕ or a minus ⊖ in the circle next to each sentence.

○ Act: Be true to yourself.

○ Say: I'll do it but don't tell anyone else.

○ Say: I don't want to upset my parents.

○ Say: No! I don't agree.

○ Think: I know this is a bad idea, but everyone else is doing it.

○ Say: Well, just this one time.

○ Say: I'm uncomfortable.

○ Act: Stand up for what you believe.

SO-CALLED FRIENDS

Why do you think some people would find a gang a good support system?

_____
_____
_____
_____
_____
_____

What kind of things do gangs pressure kids to do?

_____
_____
_____
_____

Who can help us deal with gang pressures?

At school: At home: In the community:

_____   _____   _____
_____   _____   _____
_____   _____   _____
_____   _____   _____

**Nick has a problem that he has written about in his diary.
If you could write back to him, what might you say?**

Dear Diary,

Lately some of my friends have
been bugging me to join a gang.
I like some of these guys, but
what they do when they get
together scares me. I know they
don't care about getting in
trouble, but I do. I don't want
to join a gang but they said if
I want to be friends I have to.
What can I do?

Dear Nick,

_____
_____
_____
_____
_____
_____
_____
_____

**we are
a safe
& caring
SCHOOL.**

MY SUPPORT SYSTEM QUIZ

True or False (circle the correct answer)

1) The coolest people are the ones who don't need anybody. . . . . **True / False**

2) It's not good to ask people for help because then you owe them something. . . . . **True / False**

3) Sometimes just listening can be a big help. . . . . **True / False**

4) Asking for help is a sign of strength. . . . . **True / False**

5) Knowing who can help us is a good way to be prepared for challenges. . . . . **True / False**

Multiple Choice (circle the correct answer)

6) At our Safe & Caring School:
   - **a.** supporting one another is a priority.
   - **b.** there are people and services we can go to for help.
   - **c.** it feels safe because we stand up for each other.
   - **d.** all of the above

7) Peer pressure is when:
   - **a.** you don't care what others do, and you stick to yourself.
   - **b.** you do what others say or do, even if you are uncomfortable.
   - **c.** you join in with the bullies and give someone a hard time.
   - **d.** b and c

8) Good friends:
   - **a.** leave you alone when you need help.
   - **b.** try to help solve problems.
   - **c.** bug you to join them in doing something sneaky.
   - **d.** none of the above

Fill in the Blanks

9) Good c_____ is the key to getting and r_____ support.

10) Peer p_____ can be positive or n_____.

Real-Life Writing

Somebody is trying to get a friend of yours involved in something that sounds scary, and you're afraid your friend is going to get into trouble. What can you do to help?

DECEMBER
Respect Yourself and Others

- **Community**
- **Respect**
- **Manners**

- **Communication Skills**
- **Helping Others**
- **Inclusion**

Monthly Objectives

Students will:

- learn specific ways they can be responsible members of their school community
- practice using good manners to show respect

Social Emotional Definitions

Apology: To say you are sorry (express regret) about something you did that was not right and has upset someone.

Caring: Feeling and showing concern for others.

Communication: The exchange of information, ideas, or feelings between people.

Considerate: Showing sensitivity toward the feelings of others.

Disrespectful: Not showing respect for others.

Forgiveness: The act of excusing somebody for a mistake or wrongdoing and letting go of your anger about it.

Honesty: Being truthful and sincere.

Inclusion: Accepting someone in a group.

Manners: The way you behave, good or bad, toward others.

Privacy: Having time to yourself, undisturbed by others. Keeping something confidential.

Respect: Valuing the worth of yourself and of others.

Sincerity: Expressing your true feelings.

TEACHING TIPS

- Teaching the golden rule is a priority in a safe and caring environment. To teach children to care about others, we must first teach them to care and value themselves.
- Empathy is the ability to understand, predict, and relate to someone's feelings. Without empathy, children will have a difficult time resolving problems in peaceful ways. If we cultivate empathy in children while they are young, they will grow to be empathetic adults.
- Model empathy and the golden rule as often as you can.

DECEMBER INTEGRATED ACTIVITIES

In addition to the specific lesson plans for this month, you can use these optional ideas to integrate and extend the Safe & Caring themes into your daily routines and across curricular areas.

LANGUAGE ARTS

- Students read *Hello World! Greetings in 42 Languages Around the Globe!* by Manya Stojic and identify how many greetings they know in different languages. Create a classroom list of greetings representing the diversity of the group.

- Create a classroom book with students' short stories and drawings about equality and inclusion.

- Have a special event called "Author's Day" where students read books by specific authors based on the monthly theme.

LITERATURE

- Students read books about great citizens (for example: Mother Teresa, Benito Juárez, Booker T. Washington, or Jane Addams).

- Read *The Journal of Ben Uchida* by Barry Denenberg. Twelve-year-old Ben Uchida keeps a journal of his experiences as a prisoner in a Japanese internment camp in Mirror Lake, California, during World War II.

- Establish a Book Review Day. Ask each student or a small group of students to find a creative way to present a book review to the class.

SOCIAL STUDIES

- Students work in small groups making lists of their contributions to help make their school a safe and caring place.

- Discuss the history of the community and neighborhood around your school. Explain to students that an important part of good citizenship is taking pride in and doing positive things for their community.

MATH

- Read *Mathematicians Are People, Too: Stories from the Lives of Great Mathematicians* by Luetta Reimer and Wilbert Reimer. Includes 15 illustrated vignettes that introduce students to great mathematicians from various cultures.

ART

- Students read *Inspirations: Stories About Women Artists* by Leslie Sills. Review how the four artists in the book created their art based on their own personal experiences. Students create artwork related to the monthly theme. Display their art, showcasing the uniqueness of each.

- Have students design a school bulletin board describing what it means to be respectful.

- Create posters or murals to show ways students and adults can make everyone feel a part of their school community.

SCIENCE

- Read *The 10 Things All Future Mathematicians and Scientists Must Know (But Are Rarely Taught)* by Edward Zaccaro. When we think about math and science, we usually think of calculations and facts. This book goes beyond numbers and formulas to show how math and science relate to the real world.

For an added challenge, at the end of each month, have students work individually or in small groups to create their own word find puzzles, using the words defined in "Social Emotional Definitions" (see page 77).

The Language of Respect

LEARNING OBJECTIVE

Students will:

- gain a better understanding of how their words and actions can affect other people in positive or negative ways

MATERIALS NEEDED

The book *Character Building Day by Day* by Anne D. Mather and Louise B. Weldon, "The Language of Respect" activity sheet (page 86), and pencils or pens

LESSON PLAN

CHECK IT   Ask the class: How do you feel when someone is being rude and unkind? Does it hurt people's feelings, make it harder to keep friends, or escalate conflict? Tell students that it can do all of these things.

READ IT   *Character Building Day by Day*, "Super Smart" (page 205).

DO IT   Students complete "The Language of Respect" activity sheet. Students work in small groups to rate and rewrite disrespectful phrases.

TALK ABOUT IT   Review situations where conflict may escalate because of a tone of voice, a look, or a choice of words. Remind students that they have the power to choose how they use words and actions to get along with others.

WRITE ABOUT IT   In their journals, students respond to the prompt: Write about a time when your choice of words or actions turned a situation into a conflict. Explain what went wrong and how the conflict could have been avoided.

MORE COOL READS   *Tangerine* by Edward Bloor. Living in surreal Tangerine County, Florida, a blind boy uncovers the ugly truth about his football-hero brother.

Safe & Caring Vocabulary and Word Find

LEARNING OBJECTIVES

Students will:

- be introduced to vocabulary that supports respecting yourself and others
- internalize the vocabulary as they use it throughout the month and year in real-life situations

MATERIALS NEEDED

"Safe & Caring Vocabulary" (page 84) and "Safe & Caring Word Find" (page 85) activity sheets, dictionaries, and pencils

LESSON PLAN

Use the vocabulary activities to introduce the concepts and common language associated with this month's theme. Throughout the month, use the words in writing, spelling, storytelling, and dealing with conflict situations.

For "Safe & Caring Vocabulary," explain how to use the secret code to decipher the message. (To ***create*** a safe and caring school, we must ***learn*** to ***respect*** ourselves and ***others***. Being ***rude*** does not help us get along with one another. ***Choosing*** to use good ***manners*** shows we are ***sensitive*** to how others ***feel*** and ***considerate*** of their ***rights***. We can get what we need by being ***assertive*** and ***thoughtful***. When we ***communicate*** with ***polite*** words and ***actions***, we are choosing to be assertive, not ***aggressive***.)

For "Safe & Caring Word Find," discuss what the words mean after completing the page. You may want students to work in pairs to help each other.

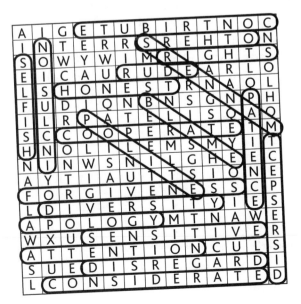

My Story of Acceptance

LEARNING OBJECTIVES

Students will:

- learn to appreciate diversity
- understand that everyone deserves equality and respect

MATERIALS NEEDED

The book *Beethoven Lives Upstairs* by Barbara Nichol, "My Story of Acceptance" activity sheet (page 87), and pencils or pens

LESSON PLAN

CHECK IT   Introduce the words *diversity* and *equality*. Ask students: What do these words mean? Is diversity celebrated and accepted in our school? What can you do to increase awareness about diversity? What does acceptance have to do with diversity?

READ IT   Read *Beethoven Lives Upstairs*. When young Christopher's family takes Ludwig van Beethoven as an upstairs tenant, their home life becomes noisy and chaotic.

DO IT   Students complete the "My Story of Acceptance" activity sheet. Students work individually to write a short story about a personal or fictional experience regarding acceptance.

TALK ABOUT IT

Students share stories. Create a classroom book of stories and include student artwork. Ask students: Have you ever been treated unfairly because of the way you look, the way you sound, your culture, your gender, or your beliefs? What happened? How did you feel about it? Why do you think it's sometimes hard for people to accept each other? Have you ever judged someone before you had a chance to get to know her or him? Have you ever excluded someone because you were pressured by your friends to do so?

WRITE ABOUT IT   In their journals, students respond to the prompt: To me, acceptance means...

MORE COOL READS   In *The Ballad of Lucy Whipple* by Karen Cushman, California Morning Whipple describes her family's move and six-year stay in a small mining town during the Gold Rush. California rebels by renaming herself Lucy. She hoards gold dust and saves the money she earns from baking pies to fund a journey home. In time Lucy realizes that home is wherever she makes one.

Don't Blame Me!

LEARNING OBJECTIVES

Students will:

- learn the importance of being responsible for their actions
- discuss how it feels to be blamed for things they have not done

MATERIALS NEEDED

The book *Character Building Day by Day* by Anne D. Mather and Louise B. Weldon, "Don't Blame Me!" activity sheet (page 88), and writing and drawing utensils

LESSON PLAN

CHECK IT   Ask students if they know what it means to be responsible for their actions. Often when students are asked who is responsible for the things they say and do, they answer, "my parents," "my teacher," or "my friends." Although this is a difficult concept, it is important to help students understand that their actions are the result of the choices they make.

READ IT   In *Character Building Day by Day*, "The Sand Sculpture" (page 125), Julio could have blamed someone else, but he didn't. He accepts responsibility for his actions.

DO IT   Students complete the "Don't Blame Me!" activity sheet, writing their own cartoon strip about blaming.

TALK ABOUT IT   Students share cartoon strips. Discuss why people choose to blame. Ask students: What are the consequences of blaming others? How does being blamed make people feel? Have you ever blamed others for your choices and behavior?

WRITE ABOUT IT   In their journals, students respond to the prompt: A time I was blamed for something I did not do...

MORE COOL READS   *Silent to the Bone* by E.L. Konigsburg is loosely based on the true story of a young mute man accused of hurting his sister.

Work It Out

LEARNING OBJECTIVES

Students will:

- learn how to apologize and forgive
- explore personal responsibility

MATERIALS NEEDED

The book *Character Building Day by Day* by Anne D. Mather and Louise B. Weldon, "Work It Out" activity sheet (page 89), and pencils or pens

LESSON PLAN

CHECK IT Ask students to explain *apology* and *forgiveness* and give examples of times when each is required. Is it ever appropriate to say "That's okay" after someone apologizes to you? Is it ever okay to hurt someone? Does an apology make the hurt go away?

READ IT *Character Building Day by Day*, "For Giving" (page 99) shows us that forgiving can make us feel better.

DO IT Complete the "Work It Out" activity sheet. Students write about a time they needed to apologize and a time they needed to accept an apology.

TALK ABOUT IT Discuss the completed activity sheets as a class. Review the steps for apologizing: (1) look at the person, (2) say it like you mean it, (3) use respectful words, and (4) come up with a plan both people can live with. Emphasize that it takes courage to apologize and to forgive each other. It's important to validate students' feelings of being upset or angry when someone treats them in a disrespectful way. To get along with others, they must learn to reciprocate with an apology and forgiveness.

WRITE ABOUT IT In their journals, students respond to the prompt: Accepting an apology is just as important as offering an apology because...

Believe Me!

LEARNING OBJECTIVES

Students will:

- explore the meaning of honesty
- discuss the consequences of being dishonest

MATERIALS NEEDED

The book *Character Building Day by Day* by Anne D. Mather and Louise B. Weldon, "Believe Me!" activity sheet (page 90), and pencils or pens

LESSON PLAN

CHECK IT

Write the words *honest* and *tactful* on the board and talk with students about the relationship between the two. Make a connection between good manners and tactfulness. Have students think about how being honest affects their relationships with others.

READ IT *Character Building Day by Day*, "Hairstyles" (page 122) addresses being honest about how something looks.

DO IT Students complete the "Believe Me!" activity sheet. Students define and write about honesty.

TALK ABOUT IT Have students share their paragraphs. Review what students learned about the benefits of being honest and the consequences of being dishonest.

WRITE ABOUT IT In their journals, students respond to the prompt: Telling the truth is not always easy, but it is important because...

MORE COOL READS *Undercover Tailback* by Matt Christopher.

Private Space

LEARNING OBJECTIVES

Students will:

- learn the meaning of privacy
- explore their needs for personal privacy and the need to respect the privacy of others

MATERIALS NEEDED

The book *Too Old for This, Too Young for That!* by Harriet S. Mosatche and Karen Unger, "Private Space" activity sheet (page 91), and pencils or pens

LESSON PLAN

CHECK IT Ask students: Is your privacy respected by your family members, friends, and others? When you give private information to a friend, is it appropriate for the friend to share that information with someone else? What if your friend feels worried or thinks you need help? Give examples. When is it okay to share private information that a friend has given you?

READ IT *Too Old for This, Too Young for That!*, "Privacy" (page 84).

DO IT Distribute and have students complete the "Private Space" activity sheet. Students create a TV commercial describing how to get some privacy.

TALK ABOUT IT Discuss key points about privacy and how it differs from secrecy. Ask students: When it is not okay to keep secrets?

WRITE ABOUT IT In their journals, students respond to the prompt: Everybody has the right to some privacy because...

Get the Facts

LEARNING OBJECTIVES

Students will:

- learn how to get the facts about a situation before they jump to a conclusion
- learn to respect each other's feelings and not spread rumors

MATERIALS NEEDED

The book *The Courage to Be Yourself* edited by Al Desetta, "Get the Facts" activity sheet (page 92), and pencils or pens

LESSON PLAN

CHECK IT Ask students if they have ever found themselves dealing with conflict because of a misunderstanding. Explain that most misunderstandings occur when people do not have the facts or do not know how to communicate effectively. Discuss how easy it is for information to be altered when transferred from one person to the next, and relate it to how quickly a rumor can spread. Ask the following questions: Have you ever jumped to conclusions before you had all the facts? What happened? How did everyone involved feel about the situation? Have you ever been blamed for something you did not do because others did not have all the facts? How did you feel about it? Do you think rumors can be hurtful? Why? What can you do to stop rumors?

READ IT *The Courage to Be Yourself*, "Nasty Girls" (pages 67–71).

DO IT Students complete the "Get the Facts" activity sheet. Students think of conflict situations that took place and record the incorrect information that started it.

TALK ABOUT IT Have students share some of their stories. Ask them to come up with ideas to help them avoid unnecessary misunderstandings.

WRITE ABOUT IT In their journals, students respond to the prompt: Something I can do to keep from making incorrect judgments is...

Good Manners

LEARNING OBJECTIVES

Students will:

- learn about manners
- consider good character traits

MATERIALS NEEDED

The book *Be the Best You Can Be* by Robin Thompson, "Good Manners" activity sheet (page 93), and pencils or pens

LESSON PLAN

CHECK IT Ask students: What are good manners? Have manners changed over the years? Make the connection between good manners and character traits like honesty, forgiveness, and respect.

READ IT *Be the Best You Can Be* is an easy-to-use guide to good manners and self-improvement. Quizzes and reviews are included in each section.

DO IT Students complete the "Good Manners" activity sheet. Students rank the list of behaviors from best to worst manners.

TALK ABOUT IT Review information from the completed activity sheets. Compare students' rankings. Ask students: How easy was it to rank the behaviors? What did you discover? Did some of you find a behavior disgusting while others did not? Was there one situation you all agreed upon? Discuss how students' behavior can make a difference in people's perceptions of them.

WRITE ABOUT IT In their journals, students respond to the prompt: Using good manners will benefit me because...

MORE COOL READS *How Rude! The Teenagers' Guide to Good Manners, Proper Behavior, and Not Grossing People Out* by Alex J. Packer is a great reference book you can use any time during the school year.

Compassion in Our Community

LEARNING OBJECTIVES

Students will:

- understand the importance of having compassion toward others
- learn specific skills that show compassion and kindness

MATERIALS NEEDED

The book *Character Building Day by Day* by Anne D. Mather and Louise B. Weldon, "Compassion in Our Community" activity sheet (page 94), pencils or pens, and dictionaries

LESSON PLAN

CHECK IT   Ask students: When someone asks us to have compassion, what do they mean? What is compassion? Relate compassion to diversity and understanding.

READ IT   In *Character Building Day by Day*, "Tears at the Table" (page 64), a friend of Donna's older brother's shows compassion toward Donna.

DO IT   Students complete the "Compassion in Our Community" activity sheet. Students define and discuss the word *compassion* in small groups. (The opposite of compassion is coldness.)

TALK ABOUT IT   Review the completed activity sheets. Discuss what actions show compassion toward others at school, in families, and within the community. Ask students: Why is it important to have compassion? What is the connection between compassion and helping others?

WRITE ABOUT IT   In their journals, students respond to either prompt: (a) Tell about a time you showed compassion toward someone who needed support or (b) Tell about a time you needed someone to show compassion toward you.

Everybody Is Welcome

LEARNING OBJECTIVES

Students will:

- examine the concept of inclusion
- determine ways to avoid excluding others

MATERIALS NEEDED

The book *The Printer* by Myron Uhlberg, "Everybody Is Welcome" activity sheet (page 95), and pencils or pens

LESSON PLAN

CHECK IT   Introduce the concept of *inclusion*. Ask students: Where do you see inclusion at home or in the classroom? Brainstorm words that are associated with inclusion.

READ IT   In *The Printer*, a story set in New York City in 1940, a young boy talks about his deaf father, who is a printer with a big daily newspaper. Dad and the other deaf workers feel isolated from their hearing colleagues, until Dad discovers a deadly fire in the factory and uses sign language to warn everyone.

DO IT   Students complete the "Everybody Is Welcome" activity sheet. Students describe inclusion and exclusion and list ways to include others at school.

TALK ABOUT IT   Discuss how people feel when they are excluded or ignored because of their gender, race, culture, or abilities. Ask students: Have you ever felt excluded? Did you ask someone for help? Did it make the situation better?

WRITE ABOUT IT   In their journals, students respond to the prompt: I can help stop exclusion by...

MORE COOL READS   In *A Corner of the Universe* by Ann M. Martin, while watching home movies, Hattie looks back over the summer of 1960 and the events that changed her perception of life. In *Bluish* by Virginia Hamilton, after Dreenie starts at a new school, she feels drawn to a frail classmate who everyone calls "Bluish."

Respect Yourself and Others Quiz

To assess student progress, use the quiz on page 96.
(*Answers: 1-T, 2-F, 3-F, 4-F, 5-T, 6-d, 7-d, 8-b, 9-respect, positive, 10-disagreements, apologize*)

Safe & Caring Vocabulary

Use the code to spell the missing words.

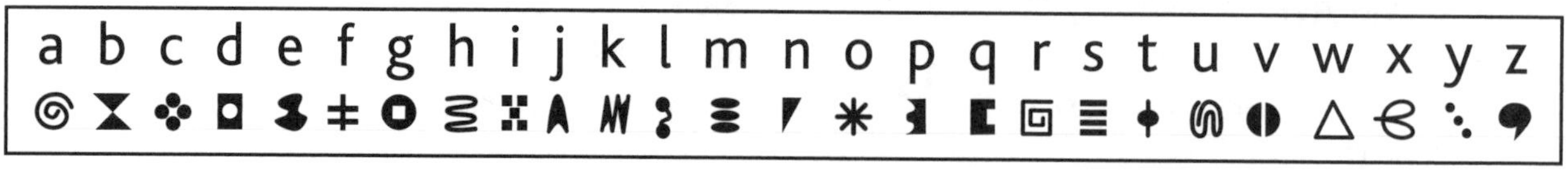

a	b	c	d	e	f	g	h	i	j	k	l	m	n	o	p	q	r	s	t	u	v	w	x	y	z
⊚	✗	✦	◻	◼	⧺	⊙	≋	⋈	▲	⋒	⦂	≋	⁊	✳	⦀	⊑	⊞	≣	✦	⌇	◑	△	⋐	⸪	❢

To _ _ _ _ _ _ a safe and caring school, we must _ _ _ _ _

to _ _ _ _ _ _ _ ourselves and _ _ _ _ _ _. Being _ _ _ _

does not help us get along with one another.

_ _ _ _ _ _ _ _ _ to use good _ _ _ _ _ _ _ shows we are

_ _ _ _ _ _ _ _ _ to how others _ _ _ _ and

_ _ _ _ _ _ _ _ _ _ of their _ _ _ _ _ _. We can get

what we need by being _ _ _ _ _ _ _ _ _ and

_ _ _ _ _ _ _ _ _ _. When we _ _ _ _ _ _ _ _ _ _ _ _ with

_ _ _ _ _ _ _ words and _ _ _ _ _ _ _, we are choosing

to be assertive, not _ _ _ _ _ _ _ _ _ _ _.

Define the word **patience**. _____

_____

_____

Write a sentence using the words **rude**, **positive**, and **cooperate**.

_____

_____

_____

we are
a safe
& caring
school.

SAFE & CARING WORD FIND

Find and circle the words listed at the bottom of the page.

(Hint: Answers can run forward, backward, up, down, or diagonally.)

A	I	G	E	T	U	B	I	R	T	N	O	C
I	N	T	E	R	R	S	R	E	H	T	O	N
S	O	W	Y	W	I	M	R	I	G	H	T	S
E	I	C	A	U	R	U	D	E	A	R	L	O
L	S	H	O	N	E	S	T	R	N	A	Q	L
F	U	D	I	Q	N	B	N	S	G	N	P	H
I	L	R	P	A	T	E	L	I	A	S	Q	A	O
S	C	C	O	O	P	E	R	M	S	T	E	T	M
H	N	I	O	L	S	L	E	M	G	H	E	E	C
N	I	N	W	S	A	N	I	L	S	I	O	N	E
A	Y	T	I	A	U	T	H	S	E	S	S	C	P
F	O	R	G	I	V	E	N	E	S	S	I	E	S
L	D	I	V	E	R	S	I	T	Y	N	A	W	E
A	P	O	L	O	G	Y	M	T	I	V	E	R	R
W	X	U	S	E	N	S	I	T	I	O	N	C	U	L	S
A	T	T	E	N	T	I	O	N	C	U	L	S
S	U	E	D	I	S	R	E	G	A	R	D	I
L	C	O	N	S	I	D	E	R	A	T	E	D

BLAME   FORGIVENESS   RIGHTS   APOLOGY

OTHERS   RUDE   HONEST   SENSITIVE

PATIENCE   COOPERATE   INCLUSION   SELFISH

CONTRIBUTE   POLITE   DISRESPECT   DISREGARD

DIVERSITY   MANNERS   CONSIDERATE   ATTENTION

we are
a safe
& caring
school.

DECEMBER

THE LANGUAGE OF RESPECT

You are a **RESPECT-ologist.** Your job is to translate the following disrespectful phrases into respectful ones.

Rate each phrase on a scale from 1 to 5, then write a more considerate way to say the same thing. Good luck!

"Get Lost! There's no room for you here!"

Circle a score

Mildly Annoying   Very Offensive
1   2   3   4   5

Respectful Translation: _____

_____

"Do what I say or I won't be your friend anymore."

Circle a score

Mildly Annoying   Very Offensive
1   2   3   4   5

Respectful Translation: _____

_____

"Don't you dare touch my things!"

Circle a score

Mildly Annoying   Very Offensive
1   2   3   4   5

Respectful Translation: _____

_____

"What are you looking at? Get out of my way."

Circle a score

Mildly Annoying   Very Offensive
1   2   3   4   5

Respectful Translation: _____

_____

we are a safe & caring school.

It's important
to respect and accept others
in our community, and include
them in what we do.

MY STORY OF ACCEPTANCE

_____

_____

_____

_____

_____

_____

_____

_____

_____

_____

_____

_____

_____

_____

_____

_____

_____

_____

_____

By _____

we are
a safe
& caring
school.

DON'T BLAME ME!

Write

Draw

Create a cartoon that shows what happens when people blame each other.

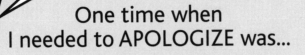

Nobody's perfect, and from time-to-time we all need to...

WORK IT OUT

One time when
I needed to APOLOGIZE was...

_____
_____
_____
_____
_____

One time when
I needed to
ACCEPT an
apology was...

_____
_____

The hardest part was...

_____
_____
_____
_____
_____
_____
_____

_____
_____
_____

I'm glad I apologized because...

_____
_____
_____
_____
_____

The hardest part was...

_____
_____
_____
_____

I'm glad I accepted the apology because...

_____
_____
_____

_____
_____
_____

we are
a safe
& caring
school.

BELIEVE me!

Define **honesty**. _____

Define **tactfulness**. _____
_____

Is honesty important? Yes ☐ No ☐ Why? _____
_____
_____

When someone is dishonest with you, how do you feel?
_____
_____
_____

When someone is honest with you, how do you feel?
_____
_____
_____

Write two paragraphs: one about how dishonesty can impact your relationships with others, and another about how honesty changes things for the better.

Dishonesty
_____
_____
_____
_____
_____
_____
_____
_____
_____

Honesty
_____
_____
_____
_____
_____
_____
_____
_____
_____

we aRe a SaFe & CaRiNG SCHOOL.

PRIVATE SPACE

People need...

...their privacy!

PRIVATE
KEEP OUT!

DECEMBER

What **privacy** means to me: _____
_____

Does your family respect your privacy? Yes ☐ No ☐ How? _____
_____

Do your friends respect your privacy? Yes ☐ No ☐ How? _____
_____

Do you respect other people's privacy? Yes ☐ No ☐ How? _____
_____

Draw and write a TV commercial about why we need privacy.

we are
a safe
& caring
SCHOOL.

GET THE FACTS

Before you jump to conclusions, be patient, ask questions, and check things out.

Conflict Situation:

Incorrect Information:

Conflict Situation:

Incorrect Information:

we are a safe & caring school.

GOOD MANNERS

Do you ever think about how some people behave in public?

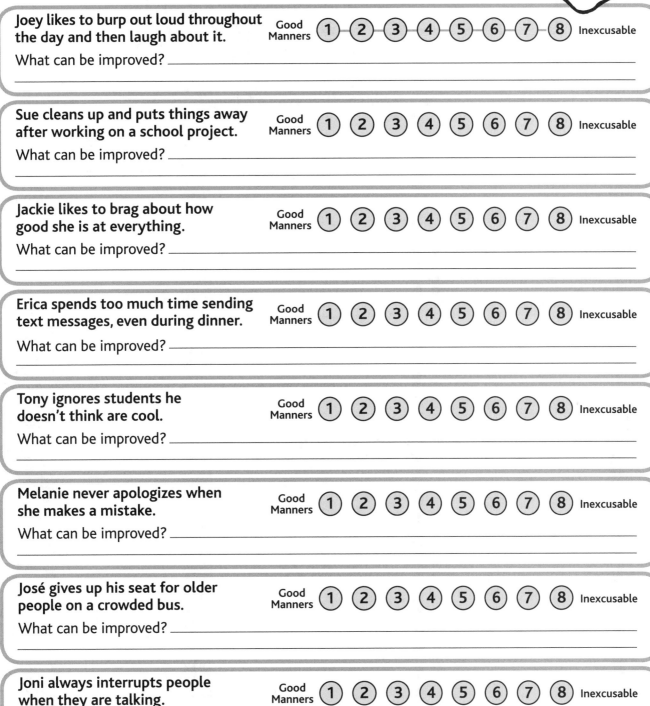

DECEMBER

Rank the following situations from 1 to 8, with 1 being the best manners and 8 the worst. Do you think the situation can be improved? If so, how?

Joey likes to burp out loud throughout the day and then laugh about it.

Good Manners (1) (2) (3) (4) (5) (6) (7) (8) Inexcusable

What can be improved? _____
_____

Sue cleans up and puts things away after working on a school project.

Good Manners (1) (2) (3) (4) (5) (6) (7) (8) Inexcusable

What can be improved? _____
_____

Jackie likes to brag about how good she is at everything.

Good Manners (1) (2) (3) (4) (5) (6) (7) (8) Inexcusable

What can be improved? _____
_____

Erica spends too much time sending text messages, even during dinner.

Good Manners (1) (2) (3) (4) (5) (6) (7) (8) Inexcusable

What can be improved? _____
_____

Tony ignores students he doesn't think are cool.

Good Manners (1) (2) (3) (4) (5) (6) (7) (8) Inexcusable

What can be improved? _____
_____

Melanie never apologizes when she makes a mistake.

Good Manners (1) (2) (3) (4) (5) (6) (7) (8) Inexcusable

What can be improved? _____
_____

José gives up his seat for older people on a crowded bus.

Good Manners (1) (2) (3) (4) (5) (6) (7) (8) Inexcusable

What can be improved? _____
_____

Joni always interrupts people when they are talking.

Good Manners (1) (2) (3) (4) (5) (6) (7) (8) Inexcusable

What can be improved? _____
_____

we are a safe & caring school.

Compassion in Our Community

Circle the words from the list below that mean *the opposite* of your definition of compassion.

indifference
sympathy
empathy
cruelty
love
mercy
tolerance
mean
callous
warmth
concern

Compassion is... _____

Draw or write how we can show compassion toward...

Family

Friends

School

Our Community

EVERYBODY IS WELCOME

When we include everyone we are a stronger group.

How would you feel if you were excluded?

Do you think others might feel that way, too? Yes ☐ No ☐ Why?_____

_____

_____

_____

Ways to include others:

_____

_____

_____

What can we do to be as inclusive as possible in our Safe & Caring School?

_____

_____

_____

_____

_____

_____

_____

_____

we aRe a saFe & CaRiNG SCHOOL.

RESPECT YOURSELF AND OTHERS QUIZ

True or False (circle the correct answer)

1) Using good manners helps when we want to be accepted by others.........................**True / False**

2) Giving others compliments isn't cool; it's silly and old-fashioned...........................**True / False**

3) If people aren't careful with their privacy, then it's fair to find out whatever I can. ....**True / False**

4) Spreading rumors and gossip is fun because you're able to do something
to somebody without really hurting them. ....**True / False**

5) Even though some things are not fair, it is still important to strive for fairness and justice. ......**True / False**

Multiple Choice (circle the correct answer)

6) At our Safe & Caring School:
   - **a.** we are respectful by accepting one another for who we are.
   - **b.** girls and boys have equal rights.
   - **c.** we create a positive place with our language and behavior.
   - **d.** all of the above

7) Gossip and rumors:
   - **a.** can be prevented when we get the facts and try to be fair.
   - **b.** aren't really serious, just having fun.
   - **c.** can have a negative effect on how kids feel at school.
   - **d.** a and c

8) Apologies are important because:
   - **a.** they can fool someone into thinking you really care.
   - **b.** they help people work out problems with each other and move on.
   - **c.** adults require you to do it.
   - **d.** none of the above

Fill in the Blanks

9) R_____ for others at school helps build a p_____ community.

10) Everyone has d_____, but we can a_____ to others, forgive them, and move on.

Real-Life Writing

At a Safe & Caring School, we are committed to including and supporting everyone.
How can you make everyone feel respected and included in the community, whether
they are boys, girls, have different abilities, or come from a different culture?

JANUARY
Bullying

- **Empathy**
- **Bullying**

- **Teasing**

Monthly Objectives

Students will:

- learn to understand and accept people because of qualities they have on the inside
- practice empathy skills as they learn the importance of compassion and kindness

Social Emotional Definitions

Apathy: Not feeling compassion or understanding toward something or someone.

Bully: An aggressive person who intimidates or mistreats others.

Compassion: Sympathy and desire to help someone in need.

Empathy: The ability to identify with and understand someone's feelings or challenges.

Ethnic Background: The group you belong to that shares distinctive cultural traits.

Intimidation: Persuading someone to do something by scaring or threatening them.

Isolation: The process of choosing to exclude someone from a group.

Judgment: The ability to form an opinion and make a decision based on one's perception.

Peer Pressure: The social pressure placed on someone to behave or dress a certain way in order to be accepted as part of a group.

Sense of Humor: The ability to laugh and see the funny side of things without hurting others.

Signal: A piece of information communicated by an action, gesture, or sign. Information the brain receives that prompts a person to act.

Teasing: To make fun of or deliberately annoy someone.

Understanding: The ability to recognize someone else's situation or point of view.

TEACHING TIPS

- In daily interaction with students, we often say, "Yes, I am listening," yet students complain that we do not really hear what they are trying to tell us. We need to listen not only with our ears but also with our hearts. When we listen with our hearts, we are better able to understand the subtle yet important messages students are trying to give us.

- Strive to be proactive and anticipate potential conflict in order to prevent disruptions in teaching and learning.

JANUARY INTEGRATED ACTIVITIES

In addition to the specific lesson plans for this month, you can use these optional ideas to integrate and extend the Safe & Caring themes into your daily routines and across curricular areas.

LANGUAGE ARTS

- Have students define and discuss the word *compassion*.

- Create a "Cool Deeds Book." Students record regularly what they have done to be positive bystanders.

- Divide students into small groups and ask each group to come up with a list of words and actions that describe *kindness, compassion, and acceptance*. Use the list to create a guide on how to deal with bullies.

- Have students write in their journals or draw a picture about a time someone showed caring and understanding toward them. Give students the option to share their journal entries in the large group.

- Discuss the meaning of New Year's resolutions. Why do people choose to make them? What kinds of resolutions do most people make? Have students create a list of their own resolutions, and relate it to setting and following through on goals.

LITERATURE

- Students read short stories about young people who contributed to society by being an everyday hero. A good resource is *What Do You Stand For? For Teens: A Guide to Building Character* by Barbara A. Lewis (pages 42–43).

- Students read books that deal with teasing and bullying behaviors. For example, *Reluctantly Alice* by Phyllis Reynolds Naylor. Have students discuss how the story relates to their personal lives.

SOCIAL STUDIES

- Students read chapters from *If You Lived at the Time of Martin Luther King* by Ellen Levine. Have students identify parts of King's life where he showed compassion, equality, acceptance, and kindness.

- Have students research and discuss in small groups important dates in the civil rights movement during the time of Martin Luther King Jr.

- Read current events on the Internet or in a newspaper about issues of bullying, its consequences, and the recommendations offered to create positive change.

ART

- Have students draw portraits of everyday heroes they admire and find inspiring.

- Using compassion and inclusion as a theme, help students decorate a bulletin board in the hallway, the cafeteria, or entryway of your school.

- Help students create kindness cards for people who have been kind to them.

- Students read *The Stranger* by Chris Van Allsburg, a great story about empathy.

MATH

- Ask students to create a chart showing how many acts of kindness they witnessed during the month. To make it more exciting, have each class in a grade level create their own chart. Compare the charts at the end of the month. Recognize all attempts to use acts of kindness.

SCIENCE

- Students research specific ways science can help us make our planet a healthier place to live. Discuss with students how they can contribute to this goal individually or as a group. Discuss how diseases are treated or eradicated.

Safe & Caring Vocabulary and Word Find

LEARNING OBJECTIVES

Students will:

- be introduced to the vocabulary that supports learning about empathy and compassion
- internalize the vocabulary as they use it throughout the month and year in real-life situations

MATERIALS NEEDED

"Safe & Caring Vocabulary" (page 104) and "Safe & Caring Word Find" (page 105) activity sheets, pencils or pens, and dictionaries

LESSON PLAN

Use the vocabulary activities to introduce the concepts and common language associated with this month's theme. Throughout the month, use the words in writing, spelling, storytelling, and dealing with conflict situations.

For "Safe & Caring Schools Vocabulary," explain how to unscramble the words to complete the paragraph and decipher the message. (*Bullying* is being deliberately and *repeatedly* mean to another *person*. A bully may *exclude* someone, spread *gossip*, intimidate, or use physical *violence*. When the *Internet*, blogs, digital *cameras*, or cell *phones* are used to bully, it is called *cyberbullying*. Sometimes there is peer *pressure* to join bullies and act in *hurtful* ways. This includes *teasing* someone who is *different* from us. A safe and caring school is a place where *bullying* is not *okay*. Everyone has equal *rights* no matter what their *gender*, age, or *ethnic* background. When we see *someone* being bullied, we can be *positive* bystanders and use *courage* and *empathy* to help others or get help from an *adult* we know and *trust*.)

For "Safe & Caring Word Find," discuss what the words mean after completing the page. You may want students to work in pairs to help each other.

For an added challenge, at the end of each month, have students work individually or in small groups to create their own word find puzzles, using the words defined in "Social Emotional Definitions" (see page 97).

Cool Enough to Care

LEARNING OBJECTIVES

Students will:

- learn about empathy
- learn the consequences of not caring about those around them

MATERIALS NEEDED

The book *Making Every Day Count* by Pamela Espeland and Elizabeth Verdick, "Cool Enough to Care" activity sheet (page 106), and pencils or pens

LESSON PLAN

CHECK IT Review what *empathy* means. Introduce the concept of empathetic listening (*the ability to listen with your heart as well as your head*). Ask students: Why would this be a good thing? Explain that the more we practice empathy, the easier it becomes to understand others.

READ IT *Making Every Day Count*, "August 6" (page 219).

DO IT Students complete the "Cool Enough to Care" activity sheet. They write what they think will happen if they care and don't care, list the words and actions that are associated with caring, and explain the meaning of the phrase: "The bridge between here and there is care."

TALK ABOUT IT Share the completed activity sheets as a class. Ask students to list the ways they show how they care for others with words and actions. Discuss the consequences of having no empathy, compassion, or understanding.

WRITE ABOUT IT In their journals, students respond to the prompt: Describe what might happen if individuals only cared about themselves.

MORE COOL READS In *The Courage to Be Yourself* edited by Al Desetta, "A Stranger in a Strange School" (pages 13–17), an immigrant teen describes the first day of school.

You and Me

LEARNING OBJECTIVES

Students will:

- compare similarities and differences between themselves and their classmates
- learn that everyone deserves to feel included, regardless of differences

MATERIALS NEEDED

The book *The Courage to Be Yourself* edited by Al Desetta, "You & Me" activity sheet (page 107), and pencils or pens

LESSON PLAN

CHECK IT Ask the students to explain and give examples of inclusion and exclusion. Ask: Where do you see these happening?

READ IT In *The Courage to Be Yourself*, "Sticking with Your Own Kind" (pages 23–27), a teen describes racism.

DO IT Students complete the "You and Me" activity sheet in pairs. Explain that part of getting to know others is observing similarities and differences beyond a person's outside appearance.

TALK ABOUT IT Ask students to share what they discovered about each other. Are we more alike than different? Understanding and celebrating our differences not only helps us get along, it makes our world a more interesting place. Discuss how everyone deserves to feel included and accepted for who they are, regardless of differences. It's important to help students experience self-acceptance so they might learn how to understand and accept others.

WRITE ABOUT IT In their journals, students respond to the prompt: Describe a time when you felt excluded by others.

MORE COOL READS *The Watsons Go to Birmingham—1963* by Christopher Paul Curtis is a fictional account of the bombing of the Sixteenth Avenue Baptist Church, seen through the eyes of a young northern black boy visiting his grandmother for the summer.

Don't Judge a Book by Its Cover!

LEARNING OBJECTIVE

Students will:

- learn the importance of getting to know people before judging them

MATERIALS NEEDED

The book *Character Building Day by Day* by Anne D. Mather and Louise B. Weldon, "Don't Judge a Book by Its Cover!" activity sheet (page 108), and pencils or pens

LESSON PLAN

CHECK IT Explain to students that understanding and accepting differences not only helps them get along with others, it expands their worlds and their chances to make new friends.

READ IT *Character Building Day by Day*, "The Spider Project" (page 38), illustrates how someone can be misjudged.

DO IT Complete the "Don't Judge a Book by Its Cover!" activity. Students write a short story about someone unfairly judged because of their looks or actions.

TALK ABOUT IT Ask students: What does the phrase, "Don't judge a book by its cover," mean? Have you ever judged someone before you got to know them? Why do you think people choose to judge each other in this way?

WRITE ABOUT IT In their journals, students respond to the prompt: How do you feel when people judge others based on appearances rather than getting to know them?

MORE COOL READS *Number the Stars* by Lois Lowry is set in Nazi-occupied Denmark in 1943. The story is about a 10-year-old girl who undertakes a dangerous mission to save her best friend.

The Other P.O.V.

LEARNING OBJECTIVES

Students will:

- learn to empathize with others
- learn how to support others who need help

MATERIALS NEEDED

The book *Character Building Day by Day* by Anne D. Mather and Louise B. Weldon, "The Other P.O.V." activity sheet (page 109), and pencils or pens

LESSON PLAN

CHECK IT Ask students: What is a point of view? How do you react when you see someone in a difficult situation or being bullied? Review ways students can give support and show empathy toward others in need. Remind them it's okay to ask adults for help.

READ IT *Character Building Day by Day*, "The Bully" (page 35).

DO IT Complete "The Other P.O.V." activity sheet. Students write about either a real or created situation. Encourage students to ask themselves the following: How would I feel if I were in a similar situation? What would I need from my friends and others around me? What if everyone chooses to look the other way? What if I try to help and I get in trouble?

TALK ABOUT IT Have the students share their stories. Discuss how we need to imagine ourselves in other people's positions to understand how they feel. Introduce the phrase, "Walk a mile in the other person's shoes." Ask: How does it relate to this discussion?

WRITE ABOUT IT In their journals, students respond to the prompt: Sometimes it's hard for me to put myself in someone else's shoes because...

MORE COOL READS In *Jake Drake, Bully Buster* by Andrew Clements, Jake has to use his smarts as well as his heart to turn himself from a Bully Magnet to Jake Drake, Bully Buster. In *Say Something* by Peggy Moss, the author gives examples of bullying and shows that being a silent bystander contributes to the problem.

Sticks & Stones

LEARNING OBJECTIVES

Students will:

- learn that name-calling and hurtful words are a form of bullying
- discuss strategies to deal with difficult situations

MATERIALS NEEDED

The book *The Courage to Be Yourself* edited by Al Desetta, "Sticks & Stones" activity sheet (page 110), and pencils or pens

LESSON PLAN

CHECK IT Ask students: Is there a connection between *discrimination* and *bullying*? How do you feel about kids who are bullied because of their ethnic background? Brainstorm reasons why kids choose to say mean things to hurt others.

READ IT In *The Courage to Be Yourself*, "Sticks and Stones" (pages 73–77), a student of Chinese heritage tells of the awful things said to her because of her ethnicity.

DO IT Students complete the "Sticks & Stones" activity sheet and discuss name-calling and hurtful words.

TALK ABOUT IT Students share their thoughts and ideas from the activity sheet. Discuss the following: Do words hurt as much as actions? Is name-calling the same as bullying? How can a bystander help someone who is the victim of name-calling or hurtful words?

WRITE ABOUT IT In their journals, students respond to the prompt: Have you ever seen anyone verbally bullied and nobody stopped to help? How did you feel? What did you choose to do?

MORE COOL READS *But Names Will Never Hurt Me* by Bernard Waber is about how Alison Wonderland learns to cope with people's response to her unusual name.

Bully Survey

LEARNING OBJECTIVES

Students will:

- identify bullying behaviors
- discuss practical, nonviolent ways to deal with bullies

MATERIALS NEEDED

The book *The Courage to Be Yourself* edited by Al Desetta, "Bully Survey" activity sheet (page 111), and pencils or pens

LESSON PLAN

CHECK IT Ask students: What is bullying? Why do people choose to bully? What types of bullying have you experienced or observed at school, at home, or in the community?

READ IT In *The Courage to Be Yourself*, "Beating the Bullies" (pages 79–83), a bully describes how he came to be one.

DO IT Students complete the "Bully Survey" activity sheet. Students record their thoughts about and knowledge of bullying.

TALK ABOUT IT Students share answers in the large group and discuss options for dealing with kids who bully. Although they are learning new skills, students might not always be able to deal with bullying problems alone. Have students identify the feelings they experience when being bullied and give ideas about what can be done to help others. Introduce the importance of being a positive bystander and using assertiveness skills to deal with bullying. Above all emphasize to students that their safety comes first.

WRITE ABOUT IT   In their journals, students respond to the prompt: Bullying is never okay and nobody deserves to be hurt. If you could bully-proof your school, what would you do?

MORE COOL READS   *Bullies Are a Pain in the Brain* by Trevor Romain is a deceptively simple approach to dealing with a difficult issue faced by millions of children every day.

A Bully Is Someone Who...

LEARNING OBJECTIVES
Students will:

- explore bully stereotypes
- learn what causes someone to bully

MATERIALS NEEDED
The book *How to Handle Bullies, Teasers, and Other Meanies* by Kate Cohen-Posey, "A Bully Is Someone Who..." activity sheet (page 112), and pencils or pens

LESSON PLAN

CHECK IT   Students work in small groups to discuss bully stereotypes (for example: only boys bully, only big kids bully). Ask students to describe why kids might choose to bully.

READ IT   *How to Handle Bullies, Teasers, and Other Meanies*, "What Makes Bullies and Teasers Tick?" (pages 9–12).

DO IT   Students complete the "A Bully Is Someone Who..." activity sheet. Students describe what they believe to be the characteristics of a bully.

TALK ABOUT IT   Students share what they believe about bullies. Remember that both students who bully and students who are bullied may be present in the class. Discuss what a bully, a bystander, and a person being bullied can choose to do.

WRITE ABOUT IT   In their journals, students respond to the prompt: What might you say to bullies to help them change their ways?

Advanced Bullyology

LEARNING OBJECTIVE
Students will:

- learn to recognize their reactions when confronted with bullying behavior

MATERIALS NEEDED
The book *Too Old for This, Too Young for That!* by Harriet S. Mosatche and Karen Unger, "Advanced Bullyology" activity sheet (page 113), and pencils or pens

LESSON PLAN

CHECK IT   Have students make a list of all the forms of bullying they have seen at school, in their neighborhoods, on TV, in movies, and so on. Discuss physical, emotional, and verbal reactions people have to negative situations (for example, if someone threatens you, your physical reaction may be that your stomach hurts; your emotional reaction may be that you grow worried and angry; your verbal reaction may be to say, "I'm not afraid of you!").

READ IT   *Too Old for This, Too Young for That!* "Bully Busting" (pages 112–114).

DO IT   Students complete the "Advanced Bullyology" activity sheet. Students look at bullying situations and determine how they might react.

TALK ABOUT IT   Have students share their activity sheets and develop a survival plan of positive ways to respond to bullying behavior.

WRITE ABOUT IT   In their journals, students respond to the prompt: What messages do you think the media sends about bullying behavior and why?

MORE COOL READS   *Nothing's Fair in Fifth Grade* by Barthe DeClements is about a 5th-grade class that finally learns to accept an overweight new student who has serious home problems.

It's Never Cool to Bully!

LEARNING OBJECTIVES
Students will:

- learn to identify bullying behavior
- explore the choices they can make when bullied

MATERIALS NEEDED
The book *Too Stressed to Think?* by Annie Fox and Ruth Kirschner, "It's Never Cool to Bully!" activity sheet (page 114), and pencils or pens

LESSON PLAN

CHECK IT   Brainstorm bullying situations as a class and help students make the connection between their feelings and how they choose to respond to bullying.

READ IT   *Too Stressed to Think?* "Surviving the Social Scene" (pages 120–124).

DO IT Complete the "It's Never Cool to Bully!" activity sheet. Ask students to describe two real-life bullying situations in a cartoon format, one that features victims and one that features bystanders.

TALK ABOUT IT Review students' cartoons. With student permission, make overhead transparencies of some of them and show the class. Discuss with students how they can bully-proof their classroom and school.

WRITE ABOUT IT In their journals, students respond to the prompt: If you were in charge of school safety, what would you suggest to help stop bullying?

MORE COOL READS *Stick Boy* by Joan T. Zeier is about Eric, who grows seven inches in a short period and becomes a misfit and the victim of bullying.

Cyberbullying

LEARNING OBJECTIVE

Students will:

- learn to identify cyberbullying behavior
- explore different ways to deal with cyberbullying

MATERIALS NEEDED

"Cyberbullying" activity sheet (page 115), Internet access, and pencils or pens

LESSON PLAN

CHECK IT Ask students: Do you know anyone who has received hate email? Tell students that this is a form of cyberbullying. Cyberbullying involves using technology to support deliberate, repeated, and hostile messages that are intended to harm others.

READ IT The Web site www.stopcyberbullying.org allows students to investigate cyberbullying and learn what to do about it.

DO IT Students complete the "Cyberbullying" activity sheet. Have students visit the Stop Cyberbullying Web site to help answer the questions.

TALK ABOUT IT Review the completed activity sheets and discuss ways students can protect themselves from cyberbullying.

WRITE ABOUT IT In their journals, students respond to the prompt: Cyberbullying is a serious issue and against the law. What would you do if you or a friend were being cyberbullied?

MORE COOL READS In *Joshua T. Bates Takes Charge* by Susan Shreve, Joshua sees his former bullies begin to bully the new boy in class.

Not Funny!

LEARNING OBJECTIVES

Students will:

- learn to identify the difference between kidding and bullying
- discuss the connection between bullying behavior and conflict

MATERIALS NEEDED

The book *More If You Had to Choose, What Would You Do?* by Sandra McLeod Humphrey, "Not Funny!" activity sheet (page 116), and pencils or pens

LESSON PLAN

CHECK IT Explain to students the difference between bullying and kidding. Bullying is hurting someone deliberately and repeatedly. Kidding is something friends do with each other, and as long as everyone is having fun, it is not harmful. Do you think kidding can ever go too far? How so?

READ IT *More If You Had to Choose, What Would You Do?*, "The Jackson Four" (pages 43–46).

DO IT Students complete the "Not Funny!" activity sheet. Students evaluate situations and determine if they are examples of kidding or bullying. They explore the connection between bullying and conflict.

TALK ABOUT IT Ask students: When do you think kidding turns into bullying? How do kids feel when they are being teased or put down by a bully? What can you do as a bystander to help out? What can you do if you are the target of bullying?

WRITE ABOUT IT In their journals, students respond to the prompt: How can teasing someone turn into a conflict?

MORE COOL READS Visit www.TeensHealth.com for more information on bullying.

Bullying Quiz

To assess student progress, use the quiz on page 117.
(Answers: 1-F, 2-T, 3-F, 4-T, 5-T, 6-d, 7-b, 8-a, 9-cyberbullying, hurt, 10-bystanders, including)

Safe & Caring Vocabulary

Unscramble the words to complete the sentences.

_____ is being deliberately and _____ mean to another
u y n l i l b g   t a p e d e l a r y

_____. A bully may _____ someone, spread _____,
s n o p r e   e d l u x e c   i s p o g s

intimidate, or use physical _____. When the _____, blogs,
                              n e l i v e c o   t i n r e t e n

digital _____, or cell _____ are used to bully, it is called
        s e c r a m a   s p e n o h

_____. Sometimes there is peer _____ to join bullies
c r e b y l i y b n u l g   e r s u p s r e

and act in _____ ways. This includes _____ someone who is
          f l u r t u h   s t i n e g a

_____ from us. A safe and caring school is a place where
t r e f n e i f d

_____ is not ____. Everyone has equal _____ no matter what
u y n l i l b g   a k o y   s t i r g h

their _____, age, or _____ background. When we see _____
      r e d n g e   c i t n e h   e m o o s e n

being bullied, we can be _____ bystanders and use _____
                        t o p e v s i i   r e g a c u o

and _____ to help others or get help from an _____ we
    y a p e m t h   l u d a t

know and _____.
        u t r t s

Define the word **empathy**. _____

_____

_____

Write a paragraph using the words **prejudice**, **stereotype**, and **understanding**.

_____

_____

_____

_____

WE ARE
A SAFE
& CARING
SCHOOL.

SAFE & CARING WORD FIND

Find and circle the words listed at the bottom of the page.

(Hint: Answers can run forward, backward, up, down, or diagonally.)

A	B	T	V	U	S	T	H	G	I	R	R	D
G	D	S	M	O	C	E	Z	U	B	E	E	E
G	I	P	D	E	O	S	T	R	U	S	T	L
R	S	B	I	B	N	K	O	J	L	P	C	I
E	A	I	S	E	F	Y	M	S	L	O	A	B
S	G	N	R	C	I	T	Z	E	Y	N	R	E
S	R	T	E	A	S	I	N	G	W	S	A	R
I	E	I	S	A	S	L	P	J	E	I	H	A
O	R	M	P	T	T	A	T	O	X	B	C	T
N	E	I	E	S	C	U	X	J	C	I	Y	E
U	D	D	C	I	E	Q	U	S	L	L	H	G
D	N	A	T	S	R	E	D	N	U	I	T	N
W	A	T	U	S	V	V	W	K	F	D	T	A
P	T	E	F	A	I	R	P	Z	E	Y	P	D
L	S	Q	O	N	F	L	I	C	T	S	M	D
E	Y	A	C	C	E	P	T	A	N	C	E	I
R	B	P	S	H	A	R	E	L	T	B	W	K
P	R	E	E	C	N	A	T	S	I	S	S	A

EQUALITY	TRUST	EMPATHY	AGGRESSION
INTIMIDATE	BYSTANDER	DISRESPECT	HELPFUL
SHARE	ASSISTANCE	CHARACTER	RIGHTS
TEASING	UNDERSTAND	RESPONSIBILITY	EXCLUDE
BULLY	DELIBERATE	ACCEPTANCE	KIDDING

we are
a safe
& CARING
SCHOOL.

JANUARY

COOL ENOUGH TO CARE

Complete these sentences

We show how we care when we...

_____
_____
_____
_____
_____

When people don't care, they...

_____
_____
_____
_____
_____

Now list words and actions that are part of your caring vision.

Words

Actions

Here

The bridge between here and there...is care.

Build a bridge by writing a paragraph using any of the words: **empathy, understanding, caring, compassion,** and **sympathy.**

There

_____
_____
_____
_____

We ARE a SAFE & CARiNG SCHOOL.

 YOU AND ME

	Similarities	Differences
Appearance Traits • Hair • Eyes • Height		
Personality Traits		
Culture & Heritage		
Family Traditions		
Favorite things we like to do		
Skills & Talents		
What we want to be when we get older		

we are
a safe
& caring
school.

DON'T JUDGE A BOOK BY ITS COVER!

Have you ever known someone who's been unfairly judged by others because of the way she or he looked, sounded, or acted? Write a short story about it.

Title

By:

we are
a safe
& caring
school.

THE OTHER P.O.V. (Point of View)

Tell a story about bullying.
Put yourself in the bullied person's shoes.

1. What happened?

2. How do you feel after being bullied?

3. What could the bully do to make things right?

4. What could I do to help with the situation?

we are
a safe
& caring
school.

STICKS & STONES

Is it true that "sticks & stones will break my bones but words will never hurt me"?

Yes ☐ No ☐ Why? _____
_____
_____
_____
_____

If we're upset or angry, do we have a right to hurt others?

Yes ☐ No ☐ Why? _____
_____
_____
_____
_____

Yes ☐ No ☐ How did you feel? _____
_____
_____
_____
_____

Have you ever been hurt by someone's words?

Unscramble the words in the phrases and use them in a paragraph below.

use odog nemarns _____
be aserivtse _____
erca **enough to** nitsle _____
shocoe **words carefully** _____
rowk **it out** _____

_____
_____
_____
_____
_____

we ARe
a safe
& CARiNG
SCHOOL.

BULLY SURVEY

What do you think of bullying?

_____
_____
_____
_____
_____

Define _bully_:

Make a list of words and phrases that describe bullying behavior.

1) _name-calling_   7) _____
2) _hitting_   8) _____
3) _____   9) _____
4) _____   10) _____
5) _____   11) _____
6) _____   12) _____

How do you feel when you see someone else being bullied?

_____
_____
_____
_____

As a bystander, what did you choose to do?

☐ Walk away.
☐ Ask for help.
☐ Tell the bully to stop.
☐ Ask the victim to join you.
☐ Ignore it.
☐ Other: _____

What can you do if _you're_ being bullied?

_____
_____
_____
_____
_____
_____

we are a safe & caring school.

A BULLY IS SOMEONE WHO...

What does a bully LOOK like?

What does a bully ACT like?

What does a bully SOUND like?

What do you think a bully thinks?

_____
_____
_____
_____
_____

How do you think a bully feels?

_____
_____
_____
_____

Describe in your own words why you think someone chooses to be a bully.

_____
_____
_____
_____
_____
_____
_____

WE ARE
A SAFE
& CARING
SCHOOL.

ADVANCED BULLYOLOGY

Let's take a closer look at what happens when people are bullied.

Fill in the blanks below.

If someone...	Physical Reaction	Emotional Reaction	Verbal Reaction	Have you ever seen this type of bullying?
calls you bad names				Yes ☐ No ☐
takes your lunch money				Yes ☐ No ☐
excludes you from group activities				Yes ☐ No ☐
takes your stuff				Yes ☐ No ☐
passes mean notes about you				Yes ☐ No ☐
threatens to hurt you				Yes ☐ No ☐
pushes you around every day				Yes ☐ No ☐
Other: _____				Yes ☐ No ☐

we are a safe & caring school.

JANURY

As a Bystander:

As a Victim:

IT'S NEVER COOL TO BULLY!

2. Here's what happened....

Here's how I felt....

Here's what I chose to do....

1. Here's what happened....

Here's how I felt....

Here's what I chose to do....

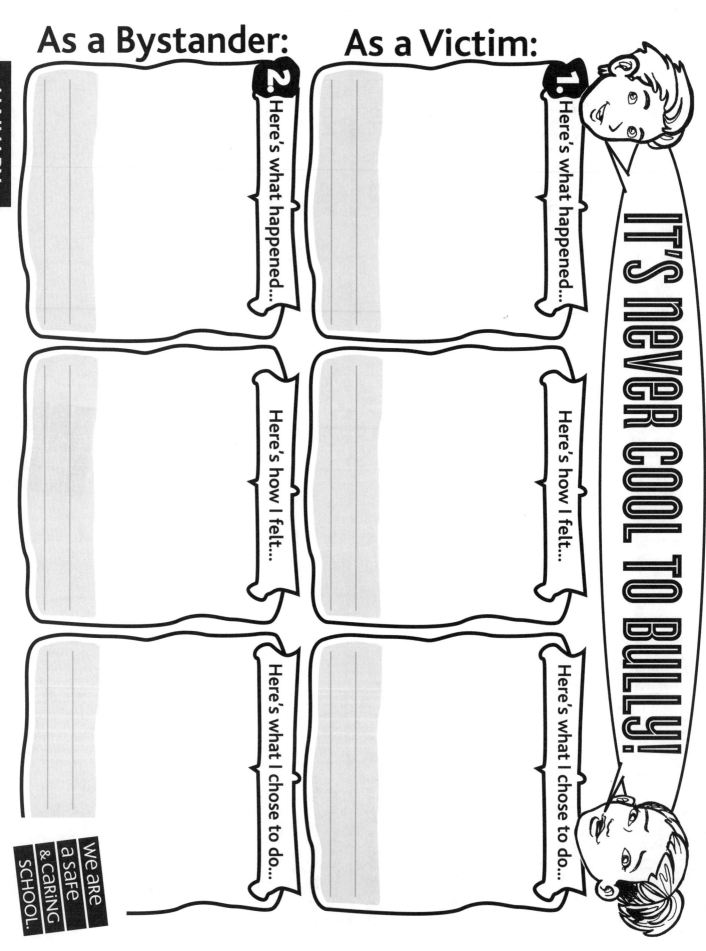

WE ARE A SAFE & CARING SCHOOL.

CYBERBULLYING

The Internet, cell phones, and digital cameras are great ways to communicate...

...but they also create lots of **ways to bully.**

What is cyberbullying?

_____
_____
_____
_____

Is cyberbullying harmful?

_____
_____
_____
_____

What are some different types of cyberbullying?

_____
_____
_____
_____

Why do some kids cyberbully?

_____
_____
_____
_____

What can we do to stay safe? List what you've learned about online safety.

_____
_____
_____
_____

Remember, cyberbullying is against the law!

**WE ARE
A SAFE
& CARING
SCHOOL.**

What is the difference between kidding and bullying?

NOT FUNNY!

_____
_____
_____
_____
_____

Let's look at a couple of examples...

The Situation

Maria accidentally knocks Jamie's books to the floor and calls Jamie clumsy, but then apologizes when Jamie gets upset.

Is it kidding or bullying?

What could you do?

_____
_____
_____
_____
_____

The Situation

Charlie makes fun of Li's accent every time he speaks. Then, Charlie posts a cartoon about immigrants on his blog.

Is it kidding or bullying?

What could you do?

_____
_____
_____
_____
_____

The Situation

Cory makes negative side comments about Chris in class when the teacher is not looking.

Is it kidding or bullying?

What could you do?

_____
_____
_____
_____
_____

What is the connection between bullying and conflict?

_____
_____
_____

we are a safe & caring school.

From _Safe & Caring Schools® Grades 6–8_ by Katia S. Petersen, Ph.D., copyright © 2008. Free Spirit Publishing Inc., Minneapolis, MN; www.freespirit.com. This page may be photocopied for individual, classroom, or small group work only. For other uses, call 800-735-7323.

BULLYING QUIZ

True or False (circle the correct answer)

1) Bullying happens everywhere, it's just something you have to put up with. . . . . **True / False**

2) When we know who can help us, we are more prepared to help others who also need support. . **True / False**

3) Girl bullies aren't as mean as boy bullies. . . . . **True / False**

4) Cyberbullying involves using technology to intimidate, threaten, or humiliate others. . . . . **True / False**

5) It takes courage and a plan to stand up to a bully, because we have to make sure
   to stay safe while we stand up for our rights. . . . . **True / False**

Multiple Choice (circle the correct answer)

6) At our Safe & Caring School:
   - **a.** we don't have to worry about bullying.
   - **b.** we learn to Stop, Think, Choose not to bully.
   - **c.** we try to understand and keep in mind how others would feel if they were bullied.
   - **d.** b and c

7) When we see someone being bullied, the best thing to do is:
   - **a.** join in with the bully.
   - **b.** try to help the victim, or if it is unsafe, get help from an adult.
   - **c.** pretend it is not happening.
   - **d.** spread the word on the Internet with a digital photo or movie.

8) Ambassadors of Peace are everyday heroes because:
   - **a.** they treat others with respect and help people get along.
   - **b.** they're the eyes and ears of the adults.
   - **c.** they know all the rules.
   - **d.** they have a certificate of recognition.

Fill in the Blanks

9) C_____ is a form of bullying that uses the Internet, cell phones, and other technology
   to h_____ others.

10) Positive b_____ can help kids who are being bullied by i_____ them
    in their group, or getting help.

Real-Life Writing

Bullying can happen on the Internet, and it can be hurtful. What would you say to someone
who thinks it is cool to use technology to spread rumors, post photos, or do other things
to bully kids at school?

we are
a safe
& caring
school.

FEBRUARY
Teaming Up for Success

- **Social Interaction Skills**
- **Responsibility**
- **Decision Making**

- **Teamwork**
- **Sharing**

Monthly Objectives

Students will:

- learn the importance of cooperation in all aspects of their lives
- practice the skills of responsibility and accountability
- learn and practice leadership and teamwork skills
- learn and practice communicating effectively with others

Social Emotional Definitions

Accountability: Taking responsibility for something you've done. Being answerable to someone.

Cooperation: The ability to work together toward a common goal.

Creativity: Using your imagination to develop new ideas.

Initiative: The ability to act and make decisions to get an important task completed.

Leadership: The ability to guide, direct, or influence people.

Responsibility: Following through with what you are expected to do.

Social Interaction: Communication or activity involving two or more people.

Teamwork: A cooperative effort by a group to complete a task.

Tolerance: The acceptance of other people's views and beliefs that may differ from your own.

Wisdom: Helpful perspective that comes from life experiences.

TEACHING TIPS

- Cooperation is one skill that takes time to teach. Being part of a team is not always easy for children, because they may have a hard time sharing, listening, taking turns, or following directions.
- There are many valuable lessons children can learn while working in large and small groups. Explain to children that they have a right to their own opinions and feelings, even if they differ from the group's.
- Use teachable moments to highlight the importance of good communication and teamwork.

FEBRUARY INTEGRATED ACTIVITIES

In addition to the specific lesson plans for this month, you can use these optional ideas to integrate and extend the Safe & Caring themes into your daily routines and across curricular areas.

LANGUAGE ARTS

- Have students make a list of the responsibilities family members have at home. Discuss the importance of sharing responsibility.
- Divide students into small groups. Ask them to create a public announcement about dependability.
- Have students create short commercials about effective communication and videotape them.
- Assign letters of the alphabet to small groups. Have students come up with words that describe good leadership (for example: assertive, confident, caring, fair, kind). Collect the words and create a "leadership alphabet."
- Have students write short stories about leadership using the words from the alphabet activity.

LITERATURE

- Have students read books about leadership. Discuss how the characters showed leadership and if it was positive or negative. Then have students rewrite, draw, or act out the story.
- Students review books on teamwork and responsibility and work in small groups to write a book synopsis and create a presentation for a Book Review Day.

SOCIAL STUDIES

- Discuss the right to vote and how groups of people decide whom to vote for.
- Invite parents as special guests to describe job responsibilities at work and to explain what it is like to be part of a team.
- Have students interview adults about what skills are necessary to complete a job when working in a team.

ART

- Students read *Here's Looking at Me: How Artists See Themselves* by Bob Raczka. Students learn about self-portraiture while discovering the key leadership skills the artists possess.
- Have students draw pictures of their various responsibilities in the classroom. Collect all pictures and create a book, choosing a title to reflect team spirit.
- Have students work in small groups to create a collage showing people using cooperation skills.

MUSIC

- Discuss with students how an orchestra's success depends on the ability of its members to work together as a team.

MATH

- Have students debate an issue. After the debate, ask students to collect data about students' opinions on the issue. Graph the data and vote on a final decision based on the results.
- Students create question cubes in small groups. Each side of the cube will contain questions about leadership skills. Groups exchange their cubes and try to answer the questions.
- Students create a graph showing the different leadership skills individual students possess. Ask students: Which skill is used most? Least? Which skills do more boys use than girls? Which skills do more girls use? Which do they both use equally?

SCIENCE

- Students work in small groups to identify different seeds and dissect them. Have them find the cotyledon, seed coat, and embryo. Discuss how the plants provide oxygen and use carbon dioxide in the photosynthesis process. Groups then compare and discuss their findings.

Safe & Caring Vocabulary and Word Find

LEARNING OBJECTIVES

Students will:

- be introduced to the vocabulary that supports learning how team up for success in a safe and caring classroom
- internalize the vocabulary as they use it throughout the month and year in real-life situations

MATERIALS NEEDED

"Safe & Caring Vocabulary" (page 125) and "Safe & Caring Word Find" (page 126) activity sheets, pencils, and dictionaries

LESSON PLAN

Use the vocabulary activities to introduce the concepts and common language associated with this month's theme. Throughout the month, use the words in writing, spelling, storytelling, and dealing with conflict situations.

For "Safe & Caring Schools Vocabulary," explain how to choose the correct word from the word bank to decipher the message. (It can be *inspiring* to be a *member* of a great team. Making a *plan* and producing *creative* results is a fun *challenge*. *Successful* teams know how to *cooperate* and *communicate* in positive ways. Members have to *depend* on each other to *collaborate* in order to *achieve* their *goals*. When team members show *responsibility* and *accountability*, they can get their *projects* done faster and produce results of which they can be *proud*.)

For "Safe & Caring Word Find," discuss what the words mean after completing the page. You may want students to work in pairs to help each other.

For an added challenge, at the end of each month, have students work individually or in small groups to create their own word find puzzles, using the words defined in "Social Emotional Definitions" (see page 118).

Team Building Brainstorm

LEARNING OBJECTIVES

Students will:

- learn how to be good team members
- practice using their cooperation skills to complete a group task

MATERIALS NEEDED

The book *Character Building Day by Day* by Anne D. Mather and Louise B. Weldon, "Team Building Brainstorm" activity sheet (page 127), and pencils or pens

LESSON PLAN

CHECK IT   Ask students to explain the meaning of *team building*.

READ IT   In *Character Building Day by Day*, "The Next One's for Us" (page 184), two girls make a good working team.

DO IT   Students complete the "Team Building Brainstorm" activity sheet in small groups.

TALK ABOUT IT   Discuss specific skills students need to be able to contribute to their group. Ask students: Why is it important to learn how to work as a team? What was the easiest and hardest part of working with your team to complete the task? What strengths do you personally bring to a team?

WRITE ABOUT IT   In their journals, students respond to the prompt: Some skills needed to be a good team member are...

MORE COOL READS   More *If You Had to Choose, What Would You Do?* by Sandra McLeod Humphrey, "Been There, Done That" (pages 11–13).

Accountability Is Awesome!

LEARNING OBJECTIVES

Students will:

- learn that responsibility and dependability are part of cooperation
- identify the situations where cooperation skills are essential

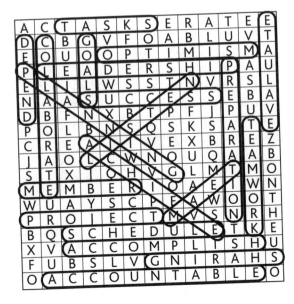

MATERIALS NEEDED

The book *Character Building Day by Day* by Anne D. Mather and Louise B. Weldon, "Accountability Is Awesome!" activity sheet (page 128), dictionaries, and pencils or pens

LESSON PLAN

CHECK IT Have students define *accountability* and *dependability*. Ask them: What do these things have to do with teamwork and cooperation?

READ IT Read *Character Building Day by Day*, "Dinner Duties" (page 66). Daughters are asked to be accountable for their actions during a dinner party.

DO IT Students complete the "Accountability Is Awesome!" activity sheet. Students record their ideas about being accountable to a group.

TALK ABOUT IT Review activity sheets. Tell students how much you appreciate it when they choose to be accountable for their own actions and cooperate in class. Brainstorm ideas about what students can do to help out at home, in their neighborhoods, and at school.

WRITE ABOUT IT In their journals, students respond to the prompt: What I like most about working in a team is _____. What I like least about working in a team is _____.

Cooperation Is Key

LEARNING OBJECTIVES

Students will:

- learn the key elements of cooperation
- compare group roles and dynamics

MATERIALS NEEDED

The book *Character Building Day by Day* by Anne D. Mather and Louise B. Weldon, "Cooperation Is Key" activity sheet (page 129), and pencils or pens

LESSON PLAN

CHECK IT Ask students: How many of you have worked in a group that did not work well together? Why didn't it work? What were the problems? Examples: Sometimes one person takes over, sometimes the group fights, and sometimes one person ends up doing all the work.

READ IT *Character Building Day by Day*, "Scrapbook Group" (page 68) shows that working together is harder than you think.

DO IT Divide students into small groups to complete the "Cooperation Is Key" activity sheet.

TALK ABOUT IT Students describe the dynamics of their group. Ask: Did everyone share the responsibility to complete the activity? Did some people take over? Did the members of your team show respect for everyone's ideas? What worked? What didn't work?

WRITE ABOUT IT In their journals, students respond to the prompt: A time I found it hard to cooperate in a group was...

MORE COOL READS *The Daffodils* by Christi Killien. When the Daffodils softball team elects a "sophisticated" new girl to lead them, former captain Nichole struggles with the growing pains of her teammates and works to prove herself a winner on and off the field.

Tracking Your Team

LEARNING OBJECTIVES

Students will:

- identify different roles used in groups to complete a project
- learn to evaluate how well their team completes a project

MATERIALS NEEDED

The book *Character Building Day by Day* by Anne D. Mather and Louise B. Weldon, "Tracking Your Team" activity sheet (page 130), "Teamwork Problem Solving Activity" directions (page 122), project supplies (listed on page 122), and pencils or pens

LESSON PLAN

CHECK IT Ask students: Can you think of the different roles people might take on when they are part of a team? Examples: leader, recorder, timekeeper, supply person.

READ IT *Character Building Day by Day*, "Team Spirit" (page 149) is about a team that needs a cheerleader.

DO IT Divide the class into small groups of no more than five students. Explain that group members will be assigned specific roles that they will use to complete a project. Using the "Tracking Your Team" activity sheet, students will evaluate how well they worked as a team. See the "Teamwork Problem Solving Activity" (page 122) for project instructions.

TALK ABOUT IT Students report their findings. Ask: Is it helpful to work on projects as a team? Is it hard to be in a group sometimes? Why? What skills did the group members use? Which skills do you wish members would have used?

WRITE ABOUT IT   In their journals, students respond to the prompt: Which role do you prefer when you work in a group?

MORE COOL READS   *The Team That Changed Baseball: Roberto Clemente and the 1971 Pittsburgh Pirates* by Bruce Markusen is the story of one of the most significant teams in the history of professional sports that included the first all-minority lineup in major league baseball.

Teamwork Problem Solving Activity (accompanies Tracking Your Team)

TIME REQUIRED

30–45 minutes

LEARNING OBJECTIVES

Students will:

- work together toward a common goal
- plan and build functional items

SUPPLIES NEEDED

Cardboard boxes (4 per team), masking tape (1 roll per team), scissors (1 pair per team), rulers (1 per team), pens or pencils

DIRECTIONS

1. Divide the group into equal teams of no more than five students each.

2. Give each team a set of supplies.

3. Instruct the teams to build a chair (or table, shelves, or other functional item) using the supplies. Give the teams a time limit and explain that they should work with their teammates to build the item, with the goal of producing the most functional item. Do not give directions on how to build the item.

4. When the time is up, tell everyone to stop working.

5. Have the teams share their planning, building, decision-making processes, and favorite or memorable moments.

6. Have teams judge each other's creations based on their functionality. Encourage the teams to try out each other's items (for example: sit on the chairs or set items on the shelves).

Cooperation

LEARNING OBJECTIVES

Students will:

- learn that they are responsible for their actions
- learn that accountability is an important part of cooperation

MATERIALS NEEDED

The book *Character Building Day by Day* by Anne D. Mather and Louise B. Weldon, "Cooperation" activity sheet (page 131), and pencils or pens

LESSON PLAN

CHECK IT   Students brainstorm different ways students can be responsible when working within a group. Discuss the importance of being accountable to oneself and to others.

READ IT   *Character Building Day by Day*, "The Secret Club" (page 69) is about a new club that has too many "wannabe" presidents.

DO IT   Form small groups and distribute the "Cooperation" activity sheet. Ask students to define *effort, organization, accountability,* and *communication*. Working in groups gives them the opportunity to practice their teamwork skills as they complete the activity. Remind students to practice listening, sharing, and respecting each other's ideas.

TALK ABOUT IT   Explain to students that as part of a team, they are responsible to share the work so things get done well and on time. It is only fair that if everyone expects to share the credit for the team's work, everyone needs to contribute. Have the teams present their plan of how to achieve their chosen goal to the large group. Discuss ways they helped each other plan. Ask students: What was easy about the planning and what was a challenge?

WRITE ABOUT IT   In their journals, students respond to the prompt: What do you think are the most challenging and the most rewarding parts of working in a team?

Leadership & Me

LEARNING OBJECTIVES

Students will:

- identify the leadership qualities they possess
- learn that great leaders also can follow and support their team

MATERIALS NEEDED

The book *Character Building Day by Day* by Anne D. Mather and Louise B. Weldon, "Leadership & Me" activity sheet (page 132), dictionaries, and pencils or pens

LESSON PLAN

CHECK IT   Students define the words *leader* and *leadership*. Ask: What characteristics are required for strong leadership?

READ IT   In *Character Building Day by Day*, "The Book Club" (page 143), Leah proves to be a good leader.

DO IT   Students complete the "Leadership & Me" activity sheet. They identify the leadership qualities they think they possess and the ones they would like to attain. Students write a story about how they can use their leadership skills in everyday situations.

TALK ABOUT IT   Have students compare the leadership characteristics they possess with the ones of the leaders who inspire them. Ask: Are there any similarities? Which skills do you hope to acquire?

WRITE ABOUT IT   In their journals, students respond to the prompt: Write about someone who inspires you to be a leader.

Team Spirit!

LEARNING OBJECTIVES

Students will:

- discuss the differences between leaders and followers

MATERIALS NEEDED

"Team Spirit!" activity sheet (page 133), "Lessons from the Geese" (this page), dictionaries, and pencils or pens

LESSON PLAN

CHECK IT   Have students define *team spirit*. Ask: Why are some teams more fun to belong to than others? What makes a team function well together?

READ IT   Students read "Lessons from the Geese."

DO IT   Distribute the "Team Spirit!" activity sheet. Students work in small groups to complete the activities.

TALK ABOUT IT   Discuss how great teams become successful because of the ability of the players to support, inspire, and motivate one another.

WRITE ABOUT IT   In their journals, students respond to the prompt: Do you see yourself as a leader or a follower? If you had the power to lead a group of people, what would you inspire them to do?

"LESSONS FROM THE GEESE" BY DR. ROBERT MCNEISH

FACT: As each goose flaps its wings, it creates an "uplift" for the birds that follow. By flying in a "V" formation, the whole flock adds 71 percent greater flying power than if each bird flew alone.

LESSON: *People who share a common direction and a sense of community can get where they are going quicker and easier, because they are traveling on the thrust of one another.*

FACT: When a goose falls out of formation, it suddenly feels the drag and resistance of flying alone. It quickly moves back into formation to take advantage of the lifting power of the bird in front of it.

LESSON: *If we have as much sense as a goose, we stay in formation with those headed where we want to go. We are willing to accept their help and give our help to others.*

FACT: When the lead goose tires, it rotates back into the formation and another goose flies to the point position.

LESSON: *It pays to take turns doing the hard tasks and sharing leadership. As with geese, people are interdependent on each other's skills, capabilities, and unique arrangements of gifts, talents, and resources.*

FACT: The geese flying in formation honk to encourage those up front to keep up their speed.

LESSON: *We need to make sure our honking is encouraging. In groups where there is encouragement, the production is much greater.*

FACT: When a goose gets sick or wounded, two geese drop out of formation and follow it down to help and protect it. They stay with it until it dies or is able to fly again. Then they join another formation or catch up with their former flock.

LESSON: *If we have as much sense as geese, we will stand by each other through the good times and the bad.*

Deciding Together as a Team

LEARNING OBJECTIVES

Students will:

- discuss how decisions are made within a group

MATERIALS NEEDED

The book *Making Every Day Count* by Pamela Espeland and Elizabeth Verdick, "Deciding Together as a Team" activity sheet (page 134), dictionaries, and pencils or pens

LESSON PLAN

CHECK IT Ask students: How do you make a decision within a group? Is it easier or harder than making one by yourself or being told what to do? Making decisions within a group requires the ability to listen and to respect others' ideas. What happens when group members don't agree on everything?

READ IT *Making Every Day Count*, "June 20" (page 172) and "December 22" (page 357).

DO IT Complete the "Deciding Together as a Team" activity sheet. Students work in small groups and discuss the challenges and benefits of making group decisions.

TALK ABOUT IT Making decisions in a group is not always easy. Ask students: Have you ever tried to convince your group to do something totally different because of your own beliefs and opinions? Do you tend to follow the decision of your group even though you disagree? Do you respect the opinions of others, or do you think your ideas are better?

WRITE ABOUT IT In their journals, students respond to the prompt: What steps help you make good decisions? Do you ever stop to think of the consequences of your decisions?

Verbal versus Nonverbal Communication

LEARNING OBJECTIVES

Students will:

- discuss the difference between verbal and nonverbal communication
- identify nonverbal cues

MATERIALS NEEDED

The book *Making Every Day Count* by Pamela Espeland and Elizabeth Verdick, index cards labeled with the following phrases (add others as you choose):

fear of being hurt by a bully
joy about passing the test
concern for a friend
sadness over the loss of a pet
anger at being left behind
sneaking a peak at your neighbor's test
pride in scoring the winning point
curiosity about the new kid in school

LESSON PLAN

CHECK IT Ask students: What does *nonverbal communication* mean? Can you describe some variations of it?

READ IT *Making Every Day Count*, "April 19" (page 110).

DO IT Students play charades using the index cards. Divide students into groups of two or three and have them act out the feelings and situations on the cards—no talking allowed, just body language and facial expressions. Sometimes words are not as important as actions. Ask: Which cards were easier to act out and to recognize? Why do you think this is?

TALK ABOUT IT Communication is composed of different methods: words, voice tone, and nonverbal cues. Of these, some are more effective in delivering a message than others. Generally, in a conversation or verbal exchange: words are somewhat effective, voice tone is more effective, and nonverbal cues are the most effective.

Nonverbal cues include: body language *(crossed arms, tense shoulders, relaxed posture)*, emotions *(smiles, frowns, grimaces, and other facial expressions)*, and the relationship between the people *(are they friends, enemies, acquaintances?)*.

Basically, what you say is not nearly as important as how you say it.

WRITE ABOUT IT In their journals, students respond to the prompt: Starting today I will use positive body language because...

Teaming Up for Success Quiz

To assess student progress, use the quiz on page 135. *(Answers: 1-T, 2-F, 3-F, 4-F, 5-T, 6-d, 7-a, 8-d, 9-difficult, goals, 10-agree, communicate)*

Safe & Caring Vocabulary

Fill in the blanks below with the correct words from the list:

plan	inspiring	goals	proud
challenge	depend	responsibility	cooperate
communicate	achieve	member	successful
accountability	creative	collaborate	projects

It can be _ _ _ _ _ _ _ _ _ _ to be a _ _ _ _ _ _ of a great team. Making

a _ _ _ _ and producing _ _ _ _ _ _ _ _ results is a fun _ _ _ _ _ _ _ _ _.

_ _ _ _ _ _ _ _ _ _ teams know how to _ _ _ _ _ _ _ _ _ and

_ _ _ _ _ _ _ _ _ _ in positive ways. Members have to _ _ _ _ _ _ on

each other to _ _ _ _ _ _ _ _ _ _ _ in order to _ _ _ _ _ _ _ their

_ _ _ _ _. When team members show _ _ _ _ _ _ _ _ _ _ _ _ _ _ and

_ _ _ _ _ _ _ _ _ _ _ _ _ _, they can get their _ _ _ _ _ _ _ _ done faster

and produce results of which they can be _ _ _ _ _.

Define the word **leadership**. _____

_____

_____

Write a paragraph using the words **innovate**, **strategy**,
and **goals**. _____

_____

_____

_____

we are
a safe
& caring
school.

SAFE & CARING WORD FIND

Find and circle the words listed at the bottom of the page.

(Hint: Answers can run forward, backward, up, down, or diagonally.)

A	C	T	A	S	K	S	E	R	A	T	E	E	E
D	C	B	G	V	F	O	A	B	L	U	V	T	
E	O	U	O	O	P	T	I	M	I	S	M	A	
P	L	E	A	D	E	R	S	H	I	P	A	U	
E	L	J	L	W	S	S	T	N	V	R	S	L	
N	A	A	S	U	C	C	E	S	S	E	B	A	
D	B	F	N	X	B	T	P	F	J	P	U	V	
P	O	L	B	N	S	Q	S	K	S	A	T	E	
C	R	E	A	I	I	V	E	X	B	R	E	Z	
J	A	O	L	C	W	N	O	U	Q	A	A	B	
S	T	X	J	Q	H	V	G	L	M	T	M	O	
M	E	M	B	E	R	I	O	A	E	I	W	N	
W	U	A	Y	S	C	P	E	A	W	O	O	T	
P	R	O	J	E	C	T	M	V	S	N	R	H	
B	Q	S	C	H	E	D	U	L	E	T	K	E	
X	V	A	C	C	O	M	P	L	I	S	H	U	
F	U	B	S	L	V	G	N	I	R	A	H	S	
O	A	C	C	O	U	N	T	A	B	L	E	O	

ACCOMPLISH	COLLABORATE	GOALS	SCHEDULE
MEMBER	SHARING	PLANNING	PREPARATION
OPTIMISM	SUCCESS	EVALUATE	LISTEN
PROJECT	ACCOUNTABLE	TEAMWORK	TASKS
DEPEND	ACHIEVE	LEADERSHIP	TEAM

we are
a safe
& caring
SCHOOL.

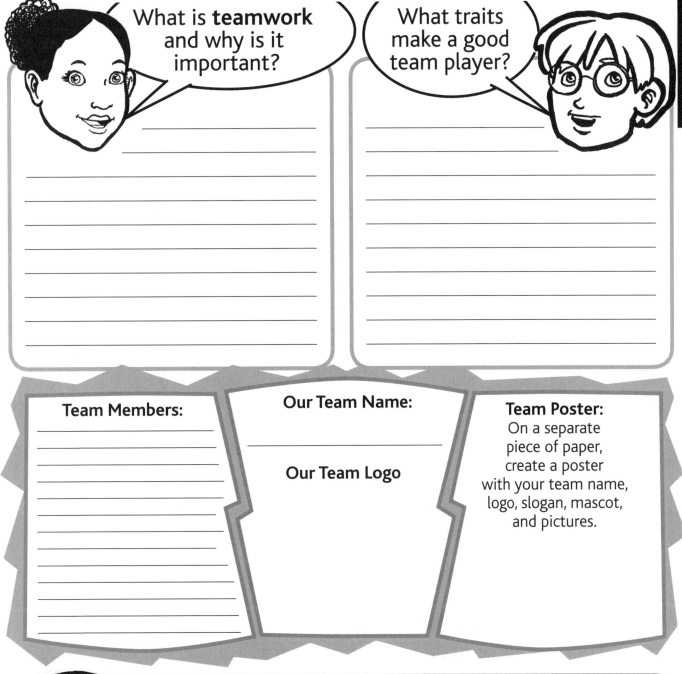

TEAM BUILDING BRAINSTORM

What is **teamwork** and why is it important?

What traits make a good team player?

Team Members:

Our Team Name:

Our Team Logo

Team Poster:
On a separate piece of paper, create a poster with your team name, logo, slogan, mascot, and pictures.

Brainstorm a service learning project to give back to your community. Make sure it uses the strengths and talents of your team members.

we are a safe & caring school.

ACCOUNTABILITY IS AWESOME!

I am accountable to my group when I...

_____
_____
_____
_____
_____

I need accountability from others because...

_____
_____
_____
_____
_____
_____

When someone says, "you will be held accountable," what does that mean?

_____
_____
_____
_____
_____

When someone chooses not to follow through and be accountable, how do you feel and what can you do about it?

_____
_____
_____
_____

I can follow through and be there for my team!

we are a safe & caring school.

COOPERATION IS KEY

A team's success depends on how well its members cooperate.

As a team, complete steps 1–6 to improve your cooperation.

6 Give an example of your team cooperating.

1 Define cooperation.

5 How well does your team cooperate?

Cooperation

2 List synonyms and antonyms of cooperation.

4 Give real-life examples of when teams don't cooperate.

3 Give real-life examples of when teams cooperate.

we ARE a SAFE & CARiNG SCHOOL.

we are
a safe
& caring
school.

Tracking your Team

Team Name

Team Members

Team Member Name / Role — Leader

Team Member Name / Role — Recorder

Team Member Name / Role — Time-Keeper

Team Member Name / Role — Supply Person

Team Member Name / Role — [add one of your own]

Team Member Name / Role

How do you think
your team did?

Team Self-Evaluation

Did your team work well together?

Yes ◯ No ◯ Explain

_____

_____

_____

_____

Our Team...

Circle
Y for yes
or
N for no

used active listening .... Y N

respected each other's
ideas and comments .... Y N

took turns talking .... Y N

set rules and worked
out issues .... Y N

divided up tasks
(leader, recorder, etc.) .... Y N

everyone did their part .... Y N

Good teams know you can't get far without...

COOPERATION

Check out the building blocks of cooperation below.

EFFORT

Definition: _____
_____
_____
_____

Use in a sentence: _____
_____
_____
_____

ORGANIZATION

Definition: _____
_____
_____
_____

Use in a sentence: _____
_____
_____
_____

ACCOUNTABILITY

Definition: _____
_____
_____
_____

Use in a sentence: _____
_____
_____
_____

COMMUNICATION

Definition: _____
_____
_____
_____

Use in a sentence: _____
_____
_____
_____

Choose a goal for your team, or make up your own.
Create a plan to help your team accomplish the goal.

- ○ A Class Celebration
- ○ A School Fund Drive
- ○ Choose Your Own

Team Plan _____
_____
_____

we are a safe & caring school.

LEADERSHIP & Me

Sometimes, you might be asked to lead...

Everyone has a leader inside of them!

Leadership Characteristics
Circle the leadership qualities you possess.
Underline the traits you WISH you had.

My Story About Being a Leader
Write a short story about one or two of the leadership characteristics you have.

able to inspire others

set a positive example

willing to take risks

follow the rules

learn from others

keep a good attitude

communicate clearly

respectful of others

give others credit

we aRe a safe & CaRiNG SCHOOL.

Team Spirit!

Working in teams helps us meet our goals. But when the work gets hard, we've got to keep each other motivated.

What does team spirit mean to you?

_____
_____
_____
_____

A team member says...   You might say...

This is way too hard!

_____
_____
_____
_____

A team member says...   You might say...

Nobody cares about my ideas.

_____
_____
_____
_____

What do these words mean to you?

inspiration

_____
_____
_____
_____
_____

motivation

_____
_____
_____
_____
_____

celebration

_____
_____
_____
_____
_____

Write a paragraph using the three words above describing how to create team spirit.

_____
_____
_____
_____
_____

we are a safe & caring school.

DECIDING TOGETHER AS A TEAM

Discuss the topics below and make decisions as a group.

It's best for us to decide things as a group.

Topic	Discuss Details	List Options	Decide Solution	Check for Success
Possible ways your school can "go green."				
Create your own:				

we are a safe & caring school.

TEAMING UP FOR SUCCESS QUIZ

True or False (circle the correct answer)

1) Teammates can achieve the same goal, even if they don't always agree with each other. . . . . . . **True / False**

2) Only certain people have leadership skills, so it's not important to try. . . . . **True / False**

3) It's cool to play games to get someone you don't like kicked off the team. . . . . **True / False**

4) I don't need to know how to work in a team, I can do everything myself. . . . . **True / False**

5) When team members have different talents and knowledge, they can find
   creative solutions to problems. . . . . **True / False**

Multiple Choice (circle the correct answer)

6) At our Safe & Caring School:
   - **a.** supportive community can help us build great teams.
   - **b.** we try to respect one another and be responsible to our team.
   - **c.** everyone can contribute their skills and talents when they work in teams.
   - **d.** all of the above

7) Decision making in teams:
   - **a.** requires cooperation.
   - **b.** can be too difficult so it is best to just go along with the crowd.
   - **c.** is the responsibility of the team leader.
   - **d.** a and c

8) Build team spirit by:
   - **a.** including everyone in a project.
   - **b.** helping members who disagree with each other work it out.
   - **c.** keeping the goal in mind and celebrating success along the way.
   - **d.** all of the above

Fill in the Blanks

9) When there is no accountability, it is more d_____ to accomplish
   our g_____ .

10) We can't always a_____ on what to do, but good teams c_____ about
    their options and try to predict what might happen.

Real-Life Writing

Your team is fun, but nobody is leading it and nothing is getting done. Someone needs to take action.
What can you do and say to help get your team moving in the right direction?

MARCH
Conflict Resolution

- **Active Listening**
- **Self-Control**

- **Respectful Communication**
- **Conflict Resolution**

Monthly Objectives

Students will:

- understand what conflict is, how it escalates, and how to respond to it assertively
- learn to use negotiating skills to resolve conflicts peacefully

Social Emotional Definitions

Active Listening: Focusing attention on someone to hear and understand the meaning of the message.

Aggressive: Having a tendency to attack or harm others.

Agreement: Sharing the opinions or ideas of another. A situation in which everyone in a group accepts the same terms.

Assertiveness: Having the confidence to state your opinion or say how you feel in a respectful way.

Compromise: To resolve a conflict by finding a solution that all members of a group can agree on.

Disagreement: Expressing a different opinion from someone, possibly leading to an argument. A situation in which everyone in a group does not accept the same terms.

Justice: Fairness and honesty in dealing with people and situations.

Problem Solving: Finding creative solutions to conflicts and disagreements.

TEACHING TIPS

- Give your students a few minutes of individual attention each day.
- Show students how to ask for attention in appropriate ways.
- Recognize children every time they make a good choice.
- Find ways to give every student a chance to succeed.

MARCH INTEGRATED ACTIVITIES

In addition to the specific lesson plans for this month, you can use these optional ideas to integrate and extend the Safe & Caring themes into your daily routines and across curricular areas.

LANGUAGE ARTS

- Have students research short stories about people around the world who made a difference by promoting peace.
- Have students write in their journals about a conflict they managed to resolve in a peaceful way.
- Assign students to watch the news or a documentary dealing with conflict. Ask them to write about everyday heroes who make a difference.

LITERATURE

- Have students create their own short stories using words or pictures to show conflicts being resolved in positive ways.
- When students visit the library, have them choose books that deal with some form of conflict.
- Have students rewrite a story about conflict and give it a peaceful ending.

SOCIAL STUDIES

- Ask students to define *conflict* and discuss the different kinds of conflict. Why does it happen at home, in neighborhoods, at school, around the country, and throughout the world?
- Read and discuss current events with students. What are some ways people can resolve conflict peacefully?

ART

- Have students create posters that show peaceful ways to deal with conflict. Display the posters in the cafeteria, hallways, or on bulletin boards throughout the school.
- Help students create collages or a mural showing the steps people need to take to work out conflicts (for example: listening, showing respect, sharing). Display the artwork in the school.

MUSIC

- Read *Story of the Orchestra: Listen While You Learn About the Instruments, the Music, and the Composers Who Wrote the Music!* by Robert Levine. An accompanying CD provides musical selections for readers to listen to at specific places in the text. These selections are short enough to keep young listeners' attention. Students read about the composers, listen to their works, and discuss how music can "tame the savage beast."

MATH

- Read *Famous Problems and Their Mathematicians* by Art Johnson, "A Promising Career Cut Short" (pages 15–17). This is a great way to spark student interest in math.

SCIENCE

- In 1876 Alexander Graham Bell patented the first telephone. Discuss how his inspiration came from his work with deaf people. Research when and how Thomas Edison developed a way for people to communicate over long distances. Study the ear, how it works, and what causes hearing loss.

Safe & Caring Vocabulary and Word Find

LEARNING OBJECTIVES

Students will:

- be introduced to vocabulary that supports learning how to get along with others and resolve conflicts
- internalize the vocabulary as they use it throughout the month and year in real-life situations

MATERIALS NEEDED

"Safe & Caring Vocabulary" (page 143) and "Safe & Caring Word Find" (page 144) activity sheets, pencils, and dictionaries

LESSON PLAN

Use the vocabulary activities to introduce the concepts and common language associated with this month's theme. Throughout the month, use the words in writing, spelling, storytelling, and dealing with conflict situations.

For "Safe & Caring Vocabulary," explain how to use the secret code to decipher the message. (*Conflict* with others is a *normal* part of life. Although conflict can be upsetting, when we *understand* how to *recognize* our anger signals, we can *practice* self-control and deal with conflict in *nonviolent* ways. It helps to understand the *difference* between being *passive*, *assertive*, and *aggressive*. A good way to *resolve* problems peacefully is to *stop*, *think*, *choose* the best *option* available. When we use active *listening* and say how we feel with *I-messages*, we can keep *disagreements* from *escalating* and resolve conflict using our words.)

For "Safe & Caring Word Find," discuss what the words mean after completing the page. You may want students to work in pairs to help each other.

For an added challenge, at the end of each month, have students work individually or in small groups to create their own word find puzzles, using the words defined in "Social Emotional Definitions" (see page 136).

All Ears

LEARNING OBJECTIVES

Students will:

- learn the steps of being an active listener
- discuss what happens when people choose not to listen and how it relates to conflict

MATERIALS NEEDED

The book *The How Rude! Handbook of Friendship & Dating Manners for Teens* by Alex J. Packer, "All Ears" activity sheet (page 145), "Totally Listening" miniposter (page 146), and pencils or pens

LESSON PLAN

CHECK IT Ask students to define *active listening*. Review the "Totally Listening" miniposter. Tell students that active listening helps us get the right information and solve problems and allows us to respond by sharing what we think and feel. Active listening provides students with tools to help resolve conflicts and get along better with others.

READ IT *The How Rude! Handbook of Friendship & Dating Manners for Teens*, "Polite Listening" (pages 24–26).

DO IT Students complete the "All Ears" activity sheet. Review the importance of paying attention when you listen to others. Ask students: How do you feel when you try to talk and nobody listens? How does active listening help us deal with conflict? What can happen when you try to solve a problem and nobody listens?

TALK ABOUT IT Review completed activity sheets. Discuss ways students can use their active listening skills. Point out that active listening includes paying close attention to the meanings of words and phrases.

WRITE ABOUT IT In their journals, students respond to the prompt: Are you a good or a not-so-good listener? What makes you think this?

MORE COOL READS *Ready-to-Use Social Skills Lessons & Activities for Grades 4–6* edited by Ruth Weltmann Begun, "Being a Good Listener" (pages 25–27).

Get the Story Right!

LEARNING OBJECTIVES

Students will:

- learn to pay attention to story details
- practice listening for accuracy and reporting what they hear

MATERIALS NEEDED

The book *Making Every Day Count* by Pamela Espeland and Elizabeth Verdick, "Get the Story Right!" activity sheet (page 147), and pencils or pens

LESSON PLAN

CHECK IT Ask students if they have a hard time remembering details about events and situations. Brainstorm why it is important to pay attention to details, especially when you hear a story.

READ IT *Making Every Day Count*, "February 7" (page 38) and "May 12" (page 133).

DO IT Students work in teams of two to complete the "Get the Story Right!" activity sheet. Divide the sheets in half. Each team member receives one of the stories. They cannot look at each other's story. One student is the reader and the other student is the listener. After reading Story #1, the reader asks the listener to verbally answer the Story Questions, as the reader fills out the Active Listening Sheet. The students then switch roles and repeat the process for Story #2.

TALK ABOUT IT Ask students whether it was harder to be a reader or a listener. Emphasize the importance of paying attention to details and reporting back accurate information. Explain that active listening—receiving, understanding, and reporting accurate information—is an important skill to learn as students communicate at home, at school, and in their community.

WRITE ABOUT IT In their journals, students respond to the prompt: How do you think relationships can be affected if someone has a hard time actively listening or remembering important details?

Imagine That!

LEARNING OBJECTIVES

Students will:

- learn about complex communication
- practice giving and following directions

MATERIALS NEEDED

The book *Character Building Day by Day* by Anne D. Mather and Louise B. Weldon, "Imagine That!" activity sheet (page 148), and pens or pencils

LESSON PLAN

CHECK IT Have students make a list of different ways people communicate (for example: via Internet, fax, TV, radio, telephone, letters, books, magazines, artwork, spoken words, sign language). Explain how clear communication is important and why we may have misunderstandings if we assume everyone comprehends what we say.

READ IT Read *Character Building Day by Day*, "Speaking Up" (page 212), and consider the issue of communicating with deaf people.

DO IT Divide students into pairs. Cut the "Imagine That!" activity sheets in half and distribute the halves to the student pairs. Have the pairs sit back-to-back. Designate one student to be the speaker and the other student to be the listener. The speaker gives directions to the listener on how to create the diagram on his or her half of the activity sheet. The listener follows the directions and tries to re-create the diagram on a separate sheet of paper without talking or asking questions. Have students switch roles and repeat the activity using the other diagram. This time, allow the listener to ask questions.

TALK ABOUT IT Have students compare their re-created diagrams with the originals. Ask: Was it easier to give or receive directions? How did you feel? Did being able to ask questions make the activity easier? What things helped the communication?

WRITE ABOUT IT In their journals, students respond to the prompt: My strongest communication skill is…

Keep Your Cool

LEARNING OBJECTIVES

Students will:

- learn the difference between passive, assertive, and aggressive behaviors
- learn the skills for behaving assertively in conflict situations

MATERIALS NEEDED

The book *Fighting Invisible Tigers* by Earl Hipp, "Keep Your Cool" activity sheet (page 149), dictionaries, and pencils or pens

LESSON PLAN

CHECK IT Review the different ways students and adults choose to treat each other during conflict. Talk about positive versus negative and respectful versus hurtful actions and words. Ask students how they feel when they are treated poorly.

READ IT *Fighting Invisible Tigers*, "Stand Up for Yourself" (pages 57–66).

DO IT Divide students into small groups. Have them define the words *passive, aggressive,* and *assertive* and complete the "Keep Your Cool" activity sheet. Students describe passive, aggressive, and assertive responses to each situation.

TALK ABOUT IT Review the three definitions. Explain that with a passive response, students choose to do and say nothing; with an aggressive response, students fight back in a negative way; and with an assertive response, students choose to say how they feel using I-messages, ask for help from someone they trust, or walk away, pointedly refusing to take part. Remind students that it takes courage to walk away from a bad situation or to ask for help. Having a plan before they act is essential to helping them resolve problems in appropriate ways.

WRITE ABOUT IT In their journals, students respond to the prompt: How does being assertive help resolve conflict and get your point across respectfully?

MORE COOL READS In *What's an Average Kid Like Me Doing Way Up Here?* by Ivy Ruckman, Norman joins with his classmates and teacher in a campaign to save Fortuna Middle School, which has been slated for closure by the school board.

Problem Solving Steps

LEARNING OBJECTIVES

Students will:

- learn the steps of problem solving
- learn the connection between choices and consequences

MATERIALS NEEDED

The book *Gandhi* by Demi, "Problem Solving Steps" activity sheet (page 150), and pencils or pens

LESSON PLAN

CHECK IT Have students define *problem solving* and ask them to make a list of the type of problems they face in their lives.

READ IT In *Gandhi*, readers follow Gandhi from his difficult, lonely education and apprenticeship in England and South Africa, through the nationwide strike he led after the Amritsar massacre, and to Independence and his eventual assassination.

DO IT Students complete the "Problem Solving Steps" activity sheet. Students record a personal problem and attempt to solve it.

TALK ABOUT IT Discuss the relationship between choices and consequences. Using the list of problems the students compiled, discuss positive solutions using the problem solving steps.

WRITE ABOUT IT In their journals, students respond to the prompt: Gandhi believed that force and violence resolved nothing. Do you believe it's possible to solve big problems in peaceful ways?

MORE COOL READS *Gandhi, Great Soul* by John B. Severance.

Problem Solving Quiz

LEARNING OBJECTIVE

Students will:

- learn how to use creative problem solving skills.

MATERIALS NEEDED

The book *Life Lists for Teens* by Pamela Espeland, "Problem Solving Quiz" activity sheet (page 151), and pencils or pens

LESSON PLAN

CHECK IT Ask students: How many times have you said to yourself, "I wish I hadn't reacted that way," or "If I could do it over, I would do it differently." Tell students that many times we don't see the flaws in our solutions until it is too late. What can we do to be better prepared for solving unexpected problems?

READ IT *Life Lists for Teens*, "10 Tips for Solving Almost Any Problem" (pages 220–221).

DO IT Students complete the "Problem Solving Quiz" activity sheet. Students respond to several situations, choose what they would do, and label the responses as passive, aggressive, or assertive. Finally, the students choose one of the situations and write the consequences of how they chose to respond to it.

TALK ABOUT IT Review quizzes. Discuss how even when we try to solve a problem positively, it doesn't always turn out the way we want. We can try our best, however, to make the best choice possible so that all parties agree with the final solution. Discuss the impact our choices have on ourselves and others.

WRITE ABOUT IT In their journals, students respond to the prompt: One of the toughest problems I've ever had to deal with was...

It's Okay to Disagree

LEARNING OBJECTIVES

Students will:

- learn that disagreements are a normal part of life
- learn respectful ways to deal with disagreements

MATERIALS NEEDED

The book *Character Building Day by Day* by Anne D. Mather and Louise B. Weldon, "It's Okay to Disagree" activity sheet (page 152), and pencils or pens

LESSON PLAN

CHECK IT Ask the class: What does it mean to "agree to disagree"? Why would anyone want to do this? How might this tactic help you when dealing with friends? Ask students to list types of disagreements they experience and describe how small disagreements can escalate into major arguments.

READ IT *Character Building Day by Day*, "Agreeing to Disagree" (page 202), show us that even best friends need to apologize sometimes.

DO IT Students complete the "It's Okay to Disagree" activity sheet. Students write about whom they disagree with and how they handle disagreement.

TALK ABOUT IT Share the activity sheets in the large group. Remind students to respect each other's opinions, even though they may not agree. It's important for adults to model this respect on a regular basis.

WRITE ABOUT IT In their journals, students respond to the prompt: Sometimes I forget that my friend has different opinions than me. To keep the peace and be respectful, I need to...

Conflict Inside Ourselves

LEARNING OBJECTIVES

Students will:

- learn that sometimes making choices is difficult
- understand the importance of being true to themselves

MATERIALS NEEDED

The book *Character Building Day by Day* by Anne D. Mather and Louise B. Weldon, "Conflict Inside Ourselves" activity sheet (page 153), and pencils or pens

LESSON PLAN

CHECK IT Ask students: What is *inner conflict?* Tell students that it occurs when we are confused and unsure about what we want to do when faced with tough decisions.

READ IT Read *Character Building Day by Day*, "Hanging Out with the Big Guys" (page 209) and "Talking to Myself" (page 210). Sometimes we have to make difficult choices. We often are harder on ourselves than we are on others.

DO IT Students complete the "Conflict Inside Ourselves" activity sheet. In several situations, students think of a positive message to respond to a negative one.

TALK ABOUT IT Discuss how students have the power to choose their response to people and situations. Students can choose to escalate or diffuse conflict.

WRITE ABOUT IT In their journals, students respond to the prompt: A time when I had the courage to talk myself into doing the right thing was...

MORE COOL READS *A Guys' Guide to Conflict, A Girls' Guide to Conflict* by Jim Gallagher and Dorothy Cavenaugh offers common-sense strategies to dealing with conflict, while exploring the feelings and reasons behind why we don't always get along. The fun, reversible design lets readers flip the book to see how guys and girls handle the same situations.

What to Do About Conflict

LEARNING OBJECTIVES

Students will:

- review the types of conflicts they experience and what starts conflict
- identify negative and positive ways to respond to conflict

MATERIALS NEEDED

The book *Too Old for This, Too Young for That!* by Harriet S. Mosatche and Karen Unger, "What to Do About Conflict" activity sheet (page 154), and pencils or pens

LESSON PLAN

CHECK IT Tell students that a conflict might begin as a misunderstanding or a simple disagreement and escalate into a major argument. Most major conflicts can be avoided if we are willing to work things out together.

READ IT *Too Old for This, Too Young for That!,* "When You're Not Getting Along" (pages 102–105).

DO IT Students complete the "What to Do About Conflict" activity sheet. Students explain what they think conflict is and why it happens. They also look at some examples of conflict and provide negative and positive ways to respond to them.

TALK ABOUT IT Students share their thoughts about how conflict is dealt with in schools, at home, in the neighborhood, and in the media. Ask if students are willing to work on positive solutions even if they don't get their way. Explain how the ability to listen, be patient, and use their sense of empathy will help students respond to conflict in positive ways.

WRITE ABOUT IT In their journals, students respond to the prompt: It is important that I keep an open mind during a conflict because...

Stop, Think, Choose a Solution

LEARNING OBJECTIVE

Students will:

- practice using the three steps of Stop, Think, Choose to resolve conflicts

MATERIALS NEEDED

The book *Life Lists for Teens* by Pamela Espeland, "Stop, Think, Choose a Solution" activity sheet (page 155), and pencils or pens

LESSON PLAN

CHECK IT Ask the students to explain the Stop, Think, Choose steps to problem solving. Tell them it takes practice to learn how to assess a situation and decide what to do about it, especially when we are angry, upset, or hurt. The more we practice, the easier it gets.

READ IT *Life Lists for Teens,* "8 Steps to Conflict Resolution" (pages 62–63).

DO IT Students complete the "Stop, Think, Choose a Solution" activity sheet. Students respond to two situations. They tell when to stop and why, what they think the problem is, what are the possible solutions, what are the possible consequences, and what their choice is to solve the problem.

TALK ABOUT IT Explain to students that conflict is everywhere. It happens all the time. Sometimes it can be frustrating or scary when we want to work things out, but the other person does not. We can only decide for ourselves how to resolve conflicts and stay out of trouble.

WRITE ABOUT IT In their journals, students respond to the prompt: Next time I find myself in a conflict situation, I will...

Conflict Resolution Quiz

To assess student progress, use the quiz on page 156. (*Answers: 1-T, 2-T, 3-F, 4-T, 5-T, 6-d, 7-b, 8-d, 9-disagree, respectful, 10-assertive, positive*)

Safe & Caring Vocabulary

Use the code to spell the missing words.

a	b	c	d	e	f	g	h	i	j	k	l	m	n	o	p	q	r	s	t	u	v	w	x	y	z
◎	✗	❖	▢	✦	ǂ	◉	⧖	Ⓧ	▲	₩	;	▤	▰	⁄	✳	⌐	▐	⌷	▤	◆	⋒	◑	△	⤸	⁖	❾

_ _ _ _ _ _ _ _ _ with others is a _ _ _ _ _ _ part of life. Although

conflict can be upsetting, when we _ _ _ _ _ _ _ _ _ _ _ how to

_ _ _ _ _ _ _ _ _ _ our anger signals, we can _ _ _ _ _ _ _ _ self-control

and deal with conflict in _ _ _ _ _ _ _ _ _ _ ways. It helps to

understand the _ _ _ _ _ _ _ _ _ _ _ between being _ _ _ _ _ _ _ _,

_ _ _ _ _ _ _ _ _, and _ _ _ _ _ _ _ _ _ _. A good way to _ _ _ _ _ _ _

problems peacefully is to _ _ _ _, _ _ _ _ _, _ _ _ _ _ _ the best

_ _ _ _ _ _ available. When we use active _ _ _ _ _ _ _ _ _ and say how

we feel with _-_ _ _ _ _ _ _ _ _, we can keep _ _ _ _ _ _ _ _ _ _ _ _ _

from _ _ _ _ _ _ _ _ _ _ and resolve conflict using our words.

Define the word **justice**. _____

_____

_____

Write a sentence using the words **negotiation, compromise,**
and **resolution.** _____

_____

_____

_____

we are
a safe
& caring
school.

MARCH

SAFE & CARING WORD FIND

Find and circle the words listed at the bottom of the page.

(Hint: Answers can run forward, backward, up, down, or diagonally.)

A	P	K	X	T	E	T	A	L	R	C	S	E
T	R	U	T	H	F	U	L	N	E	S	S	U
Q	A	F	B	O	A	R	U	X	S	W	O	O
K	C	J	K	H	I	B	K	E	O	A	L	I
W	T	A	U	Q	R	H	I	T	L	G	U	N
L	I	S	T	E	N	E	R	A	U	T	I	T
O	C	S	O	U	E	F	Q	L	T	R	I	E
Y	E	E	D	C	S	H	J	A	I	E	O	R
A	R	Z	O	S	S	A	Z	C	O	S	N	R
L	C	T	J	U	M	B	W	S	N	S	R	U
T	N	I	P	R	O	B	L	E	M	I	E	P
Y	E	V	P	A	S	S	I	V	E	V	S	T
J	L	E	B	G	K	H	U	B	X	E	T	O
F	O	I	M	E	S	S	A	G	E	F	R	A
U	I	X	F	A	F	K	Z	O	Q	J	A	Z
E	V	L	O	S	E	R	O	A	B	X	I	E
J	N	E	G	O	T	I	A	T	I	O	N	P
C	O	M	P	R	O	M	I	S	E	U	T	O

RESTRAINT	NEGOTIATION	LOYALTY	PASSIVE
TRUTHFULNESS	ASSERTIVE	INTERRUPT	I MESSAGE
RESOLUTION	ESCALATE	FAIRNESS	RESOLVE
COMPROMISE	COURAGE	PROBLEM	LISTENER
PRACTICE	AGGRESSIVE	SOLUTION	VIOLENCE

we are
a safe
& caring
SCHOOL.

ALL EARS

I think active listening is important because...

_____
_____
_____
_____
_____

Three things I can do to be a better listener are...

1) _____
_____

2) _____
_____

3) _____
_____

True or False:

	T	F
Interrupting helps listening	☐	☐
Paying attention shows respect..	☐	☐
Everyone is a good listener	☐	☐
You don't need to listen to do well at school...	☐	☐
There's no need to listen to directions to do things right..............................	☐	☐

Write about a time it would have been helpful for you to be a better listener.

_____
_____
_____
_____

we are a safe & caring school.

TOTALLY LISTENING

I look at the person who is speaking to me.

I pay attention and show respect.

I don't interrupt.

I ask questions to understand and participate.

GET THE STORY RIGHT!

Story #1:

Jason and Mark planned to go to the mall to see a movie Saturday afternoon. Jason called Mark right after lunch to remind him to meet at the movie theater at 1:00 p.m. by the ticket booth. Mark arrived early so he could buy snacks. He bought one large popcorn, two sodas, and a pack of gum. By the time Mark met Jason, Jason had bought the tickets so Mark paid him back $6.00.

Story #1 Questions:

1) Where and on what day did Jason and Mark decide to go to the movies?
2) Why did Mark go to the theater early?
3) What time did they agree to meet?
4) What snacks did Mark get?
5) How much were the tickets?

Active Listening Questions for Story #1

Listener's Name: _____

Answers:

1) _____
2) _____
3) _____
4) _____
5) _____

Did the listener...

☐ face the speaker?
☐ pay attention?
☐ listen without interrupting?
☐ remember story details correctly?

Story #2:

Natalie and Alexia met Maria after school to work on their science project. Natalie brought markers and glue. Alexia brought a piece of poster board. Maria brought her laptop computer and snacks. They worked for three hours and then stopped for a pizza break.

Story #2 Questions:

1) Why did Natalie, Alexia, and Maria get together?
2) When did they meet?
3) What did each student bring to their meeting?
4) How long did they work?
5) What did they do for their break?

Active Listening Questions for Story #2

Listener's Name: _____

Answers:

1) _____
2) _____
3) _____
4) _____
5) _____

Did the listener...

☐ face the speaker?
☐ pay attention?
☐ listen without interrupting?
☐ remember story details correctly?

we are a safe & caring school.

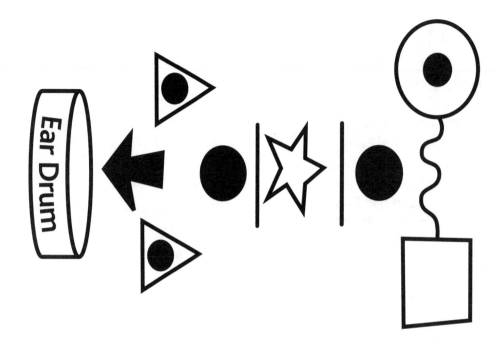

Ear Drum

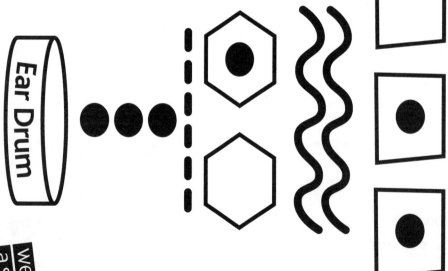

Ear Drum

imagine that!

We are
a safe
& caring
school.

KEEP YOUR COOL

we are a safe a caring & school.

Situation	Passive Response	Aggressive Response	Assertive Response
You need the computer to finish your project for the next day, but your brother or sister refuses to give you a turn.			
A friend borrowed your favorite CD and lost it.			
You were up late watching a video and did not finish your homework, so your teacher gives you an incomplete.			
Someone else talks during a test and you get blamed for it unfairly.			

MARCH

149

PROBLEM SOLVING STEPS

Describe the problem: _____

_____

_____

_____

Hey!
Conflicts and
tough situations
come up.
When they do,
it's good to know
some problem
solving steps.

How do I feel? _____

_____

_____

_____

_____

How do I think the other people involved feel?

_____

_____

_____

_____

What can I choose to do? _____

_____

_____

_____

What are the consequences of my choices?

_____

_____

_____

_____

My final plan is... _____

_____

_____

_____

we aRe
a safe
& CaRiNG
SCHOOL.

PROBLEM SOLVING QUIZ

Choose the way you would respond to each situation by circling a, b, c, or d. Then label each choice as passive, aggressive, or assertive on the blank line.

1. A group of friends decides to exclude you from an activity. You decide to...

a) do nothing ___passive___

b) yell at them _____

c) tell them how you feel _____

d) never talk to them again _____

2. Someone is spreading rumors about you. You decide to...

a) get angry and spread rumors about him or her _____

b) tell someone you know and trust _____

c) write a note to let the person know how you feel _____

d) say nothing and hope it stops _____

e) set up a time to talk _____

f) b, c, or e _____

3. A friend let you borrow a DVD and you lost it. You decide to...

a) tell the truth _____

b) lie and say you gave it back already _____

c) blame your brother or sister _____

d) offer to pay for it _____

e) both a and d _____

4. You share a secret with a friend and you now discover that everyone knows. You decide to...

a) ignore everybody _____

b) get angry and walk away _____

c) find the right time to talk to your friend _____

d) tell everyone what they heard was not true _____

Choose one of the situations above and describe the possible consequences of your choice.

Consequences for THEM

Consequences for ME

MARCH

IT'S OKAY TO DISAGREE

To me, a disagreement is... _____

_____

_____

_____

_____

	Yes	No
Parents...	☐	☐
Teachers..	☐	☐
Coaches...	☐	☐
Friends	☐	☐
Others..	☐	☐

Do you ever have disagreements with your...

Who and why? _____

_____

How do you deal with disagreements?

When others disagree with you, do you stand up for what you believe in?

Yes ____ No ____ Why? ____

_____

_____

_____

_____

_____

_____

_____

_____

_____

_____

we are a safe & caring school.

CONFLICT INSIDE OURSELVES

Ever had a hard time knowing whether you feel positive or negative about yourself? When things are hard, we need to tell ourselves positive messages so we can make good choices.

Write a positive message to answer each negative one below.

Situation: Being Included

− If I had the right kind of clothes, other kids would invite me to join them.

+

Situation: Choosing Teams

− Nobody picks me because I'm terrible at sports!

+

Situation: Good Grades

− Someone called me "brainiac" today. Maybe I should stop getting good grades.

+

Situation: Loss of a Friend

− Alex says he doesn't want to hang out with me because I won't smoke. I'm such a loser.

+

To me, it's important to stay true to myself because... _____

_____

_____

we are a safe & caring school.

WHAT TO DO ABOUT CONFLICT

Nobody likes conflict, but it happens. Knowing how to deal with conflict helps us all get along.

Define conflict. _____

Examples of conflict:

At School:
8th graders rule the halls and push 6th graders out of their way.

In the Neighborhood:
A group of students is bullying the younger kids at the bus stop.

In the Media:
The news shows a group of people carrying signs and shouting to close down a certain business.

A possible NEGATIVE response:

A possible POSITIVE response:

WE ARE a SAFE & CARING SCHOOL.

STOP, THINK, CHOOSE a SOLUTION

Think about these two conflict situations. Find the best answer.

Situation 1:

Ramon and Pete have been best friends for years. Now Ramon feels excluded because Pete is hanging out with a different group of students.

1. Stop: _____
_____
_____

2. Think: _____
_____
_____

3. Choose: _____
_____
_____

Situation 2: (write your own)

_____
_____
_____
_____

1. Stop: _____
_____
_____

2. Think: _____
_____
_____

3. Choose: _____
_____
_____

STOP
Calm down and breathe deeply.
Consider everyone's feelings.

THINK
What is the problem? What are your options?
What are the consequences of your actions?

CHOOSE
Make your choice.
Talk to someone you trust for support.

Use Stop, Think, Choose to resolve conflicts.

we aRe a safe & CaRiNG SCHOOL.

CONFLICT RESOLUTION QUIZ

True or False (circle the correct answer)

1) When we have a conflict, we can Stop, Think, Choose to find the best solution. . . . . **True / False**

2) Sometimes we can have a good attitude, and other times we can have a negative attitude. . . . . **True / False**

3) I'm used to doing lots of things at once, so I don't need to stop and listen to someone giving important information. . . . . **True / False**

4) Learning to be assertive in conflicts takes courage, and sometimes we need to get help. . . . . . . **True / False**

5) When we have conflicts, it is important to consider whether our attitude is helping the situation. . . . . **True / False**

Multiple Choice (circle the correct answer)

6) At our Safe & Caring School:
   - **a.** we know conflicts are a normal part of life.
   - **b.** everybody follows the rules perfectly all the time.
   - **c.** getting along with each other is a priority, so we practice conflict resolution.
   - **d.** a and c

7) Conflicts can be resolved when we:
   - **a.** get our way.
   - **b.** are assertive about how we feel and what we need to make things right.
   - **c.** stop worrying about how the other person is feeling.
   - **d.** b and c

8) When we are torn in two directions about what to do in a conflict:
   - **a.** we can feel stressed out and exhausted.
   - **b.** it is good to use Stop, Think, Choose to give ourselves the time to work it out.
   - **c.** we can reach out to our support system to help us.
   - **d.** all of the above

Fill in the Blanks

9) It's okay to d_____, and we can still be r_____.

10) When we stand up for ourselves we are being a_____, which can help us resolve conflicts in a p_____ way.

Real-Life Writing

It can be hard to do things we want to do if we feel bad about ourselves and tell ourselves negative things. Think of something you'd really like to accomplish. Write about the goal, what it means to you, and the positive things you need to believe about yourself to reach your goal.

we are
a safe
& caring
school.

APRIL
The Power to Choose

- **Making Choices**
- **Consequences**
- **Peer Pressure**

Monthly Objectives

Students will:

- learn about the importance of making good choices
- learn what it means to be responsible for their actions
- practice treating people with fairness and respect

Social Emotional Definitions

Choice: Options you can select in a situation.

Common Sense: Using good judgment to make wise choices.

Conflict: A disagreement between people because of differing ideas, principles, desires, or needs.

Consequences: The results, good or bad, of your actions.

Critical Thinking: The ability to research, judge, and choose the best option.

Impulse: A sudden desire to do something.

Misunderstanding: A failure to understand or correctly interpret something or someone.

TEACHING TIPS

- The key sources of anger in children are stress, frustration, feeling rejected, and feeling isolated.
- Anger is a normal human emotion.
- Teach students how to manage anger and channel its energy in productive ways.
- Children need to learn they have the power to respond to conflict in constructive ways.
- Violence is a learned behavior. With practice and positive reinforcement, students can learn to manage their anger and make better choices.

APRIL INTEGRATED ACTIVITIES

In addition to the specific lesson plans for this month, you can use these optional ideas to integrate and extend the Safe & Caring themes into your daily routines and across curricular areas.

LANGUAGE ARTS

- Have students write in their journals about choices, consequences, justice, and fairness.

- Have students work in small groups to create a 60-second public service announcement about having the power to choose and why it's cool to stand up for what you believe in.

- Ask students to write short stories or poems that explore their feelings about justice and fairness.

- Have students create short skits about choices and consequences.

LITERATURE

- Students read *The House of Sixty Fathers* by Meindert Dejong. A vividly realistic story about young Tien Pao's journey to find his family during the Japanese invasion of China. Working in small groups, students explore each character to discover how they behaved toward one another.

- Students read *Make Four Million Dollars by Next Thursday!* by Stephen Manes. Jason Nozzle is looking for his lost pocket money when he happens upon a book by Dr. K. Pinkerton Silverfish that attempts to teach readers how to become exceedingly wealthy.

- Create a list of students' favorite books corresponding to the monthly themes. Add to the list as you explore each topic.

SOCIAL STUDIES

- Students define *justice* and make a list of what they see or hear in the news media regarding justice.

- Students define *fairness* and research people, past or present, who have been celebrated for their fairness.

- Have students choose a historical figure whose greatest characteristics involved justice and fairness. Ask them to assume the role of that individual and share key facts about his or her life and personality with the large group.

- Have students create a timeline of the most important choices they have made so far in their lives and the choices they expect to make in the future.

ART

- Have students create a "Wall of Respect" by drawing pictures, cartoons, or posters portraying one of the character traits from this month's theme.

- Create a classroom book called "Making Good Choices." Ask each student to create a page for the book. These may include drawings, poetry, short stories, or facts about character traits that are essential to making good choices.

- Have students create cartoons about choices and consequences.

MATH

- Help students create graphs depicting how many classmates have made positive choices, shown fairness, or were able to stand up for their rights in a respectful way.

SCIENCE

- Students research and discuss positive versus negative choices humans make in trying to save our planet. Hold an Earth Day celebration and invite parents to attend and learn about the students' findings. Plant trees in small groups of students or families.

Safe & Caring Vocabulary and Word Find

LEARNING OBJECTIVES

Students will:

- be introduced to the vocabulary that supports understanding they have the power to choose how they respond to others
- internalize the vocabulary as they use it throughout the month and year in real-life situations

MATERIALS NEEDED

"Safe & Caring Vocabulary" (page 164) and "Safe & Caring Word Find" (page 165) activity sheets, pencils, and dictionaries

LESSON PLAN

Use the vocabulary activities to introduce the concepts and common language associated with this month's theme. Throughout the month, use the words in writing, spelling, storytelling, and dealing with conflict situations.

For "Safe & Caring Schools Vocabulary," explain how to fill in the blanks to decipher the message. (**Life** is full of **choices**. Some choices are **easy** to make and just need **common sense**, but others are **tough** and require you to **determine** the **facts**. Choices have **consequences** that can **affect** you and others around you. It is important to **predict** what might happen instead of acting on **impulse** without careful **consideration**. **Stop** and **think** about the **problem**, how you feel about it, and then weigh the **different** choices you have. If you need **help**, ask someone you **know** and **trust** for **support**.)

```
A G R I T R P F O G U R O
U A L T E R N A T I V E Y
O C B H D I X C Y H R F T
P C H O I C E T T O E L I
R O U R S O U S S E R C L
E W N C B L G E X N C I B
C U E E N H O N B E T O I
T N N R E E D O M U O S N
O T T N B R L H Q O L S O
M A E N E G A T I V E R P
E B B H C B I G L S S A S
N I R G U R I B X N A O E
D L E C I I S U Q O N C R
A I T G N R O H I R E C A
T Y Y R E V A R B O R E B
I P R E D I C T I O N N A
O E R U S S E R P T R S B
N O I T A N I G A M I G O
```

For "Safe & Caring Word Find," discuss what the words mean after completing the page. You may want students to work in pairs to help each other.

For an added challenge, at the end of each month, have students work individually or in small groups to create their own word find puzzles, using the words defined in "Social Emotional Definitions" (see page 157).

I Have the Power to Choose

LEARNING OBJECTIVES

Students will:

- understand that they are responsible for their actions and the consequences of their choices
- learn that they can choose how to respond when people treat them unfairly

MATERIALS NEEDED

The book *Too Stressed to Think?* by Annie Fox and Ruth Kirschner, "I Have the Power to Choose" activity sheet (page 166), and pencils or pens

LESSON PLAN

CHECK IT Ask students: Have you ever felt angry, sad, or frustrated when responding to an event? How does that affect the decision-making process? Would you say you make wise decisions in those cases? Remind them that even when they feel angry, sad, or frustrated, they still can choose what to do with their feelings and are responsible for their own actions (for example, if someone chooses to tease them, they can choose to ignore it, walk away, say "stop," or ask for help).

READ IT *Too Stressed to Think?*, "Tool #4: Choosing" (pages 61–66).

DO IT Students complete the "I Have the Power to Choose" activity sheet. Students brainstorm different real-life conflict situations where students need to make choices, respond to the situations presented, and then fill in their own situation.

TALK ABOUT IT Students share and compare their responses on the activity sheet.

WRITE ABOUT IT In their journals, students respond to the prompt: Explain what it means to have the power to choose.

MORE COOL READS *If You Had to Choose, What Would You Do?* by Sandra McLeod Humphrey (pages 11–13).

Targeting Good Choices

LEARNING OBJECTIVE

Students will:

- learn to recognize that stress can affect their decision-making process

MATERIALS NEEDED

The book *Too Stressed to Think?* by Annie Fox and Ruth Kirschner, "Targeting Good Choices" activity sheet (page 167), and pencils or pens

LESSON PLAN

CHECK IT Ask students if they ever have a difficult time making appropriate choices when they feel stress. Brainstorm a list of stressful situations.

READ IT *Too Stressed to Think?*, "You Still Have Choices" (pages 16–17).

DO IT Students complete the "Targeting Good Choices" activity sheet. Students zero in on positive and negative responses to stress.

TALK ABOUT IT Share answers from the activity sheet. Validate students' feelings and compare the types of stress individuals feel and how they respond to each situation. Encourage them to talk to someone before they become overwhelmed by stress.

WRITE ABOUT IT In their journals, students respond to the prompt: Life is full of tough choices. Write about a time you felt stressed and had a hard time deciding what to do.

Who Is in Charge of You?

LEARNING OBJECTIVE

Students will:

- learn about taking responsibility for their actions

MATERIALS NEEDED

The book *Character Building Day by Day* by Anne D. Mather and Louise B. Weldon, "Who Is in Charge of You?" activity sheet (page 168), and pencils or pens

LESSON PLAN

CHECK IT Ask students to explain the meaning of the phrase, "taking responsibility for our actions." Ask students: Have there been times when you blamed someone else for something you did instead of taking responsibility for your actions? Have you ever been blamed for something you did not do? How did you feel about it?

READ IT *Character Building Day by Day*, "The Big Eraser" (page 216).

DO IT Students complete the "Who Is in Charge of You?" activity sheet. Students write a story about someone dealing with peer pressure.

TALK ABOUT IT Ask for volunteers to share their stories. Ask: What's the toughest part about taking responsibility for your actions? Do you always know what you should do? How does responsibility relate to conflict? How can you be honest and keep your friends at the same time?

WRITE ABOUT IT In their journals, students respond to the prompt: How do courage and responsibility relate to each other? Can you be courageous when you take responsibility for yourself?

MORE COOL READS *If You Had to Choose, What Would You Do?* by Sandra McLeod Humphrey (pages 81–83).

Making Positive Choices

LEARNING OBJECTIVES

Students will:

- understand that every choice has a positive or negative consequence
- learn that they can change their behavior to experience positive consequences

MATERIALS NEEDED

The book *The Courage to Be Yourself* edited by Al Desetta, "Making Positive Choices" activity sheet (page 169), and pencils or pens

LESSON PLAN

CHECK IT Discuss with students the connection between feelings, actions, and consequences. For example: I feel angry (feeling). I choose to hit (action). I get in trouble (consequence). Brainstorm and make a list of choices students have to make on a regular basis, especially when faced with a challenge.

READ IT *The Courage to Be Yourself*, "It Ain't Easy Being Hard" (pages 85–87).

DO IT Students complete the "Making Positive Choices" activity sheet. Students respond to various situations.

TALK ABOUT IT Students share their activity sheets in the large group. If some students respond with negative choices, walk them through changing their choice to experience a positive consequence. Ask students to think of reasons why students give in to peer pressure, instead of choosing to stand up for what they believe in.

WRITE ABOUT IT In their journals, students respond to the prompt: Sometimes I find it hard to make a good choice because...

MORE COOL READS *The Homework Machine* by Dan Gutman is a story about friendship, honesty, and the consequences of characters' choices.

Wheel of Choices

LEARNING OBJECTIVE

Students will:

- practice making positive choices in response to conflict

MATERIALS NEEDED

The book *The Courage to Be Yourself* edited by Al Desetta, "Wheel of Choices" activity sheet (page 170), scissors, paper fasteners, card stock or paper plates, and pencils or pens

LESSON PLAN

CHECK IT Brainstorm a list of conflicts that take place in your school or classroom every day.

READ IT *The Courage to Be Yourself*, "Lighten Up on Heavy People" (pages 37–38).

DO IT Cut out and assemble the "Wheel of Choices" on the activity sheets. Divide students into small groups and give one wheel to each group. Students use the wheel to practice making positive choices in different situations. Have one student in each group record the answers the other students give.

Directions: Students take turns spinning the wheel to land on a category. The spinner then gives an example of a conflict situation for the category. (For example, for "Gossiping," the student could say, "If someone is spreading rumors about me, I choose to...") The recorder writes down the conflict situation and the student's choice of how to deal with it.

TALK ABOUT IT Discuss in the large group the conflict situations and choices made during the activity. Review each situation for acceptable and respectful responses to conflict.

WRITE ABOUT IT In their journals, students respond to the prompt: Using good judgment to deal with conflict means...

Learning from Our Choices

LEARNING OBJECTIVE

Students will:

- review consequences of their choices

MATERIALS NEEDED

The book *Stick Up for Yourself!* by Gershen Kaufman, Lev Raphael, and Pamela Espeland, "Learning from Our Choices" activity sheet (page 171), and pencils or pens

LESSON PLAN

CHECK IT Review with students what it means for them to be responsible for their actions. Ask students: Do you feel you have the power to stay out of trouble? Do you think about how your choices will affect others? Have you ever felt pressured to make a choice you didn't agree with? If so, what could you have done differently?

READ IT Read *Stick Up for Yourself!*, "Make Choices" (pages 16–18). We are responsible for our behaviors and we can make choices about them.

DO IT Distribute and have students complete the "Learning from Our Choices" activity. Use this activity as a writing assignment to help students understand the connection between choices and consequences.

TALK ABOUT IT Have students share their answers to the questions on the activity sheet in the large group. Discuss the process of making good versus poor choices, especially when faced with negative peer pressure. Then, as a group, create a list of tips for making positive choices, based on students' answers to the final question on the activity sheet.

WRITE ABOUT IT In their journals, students respond to the prompt: Write about a positive choice you have made and the results of that choice. Did you make the choice on your own, or did someone help you? If so, who helped you?

Choice Week

LEARNING OBJECTIVES

Students will:

- learn how to keep track of important choices they make
- understand the importance of personal accountability

MATERIALS NEEDED

The book *If You Had to Choose, What Would You Do?* by Sandra McLeod Humphrey, "Choice Week" activity sheet (page 172), and pencils or pens

LESSON PLAN

CHECK IT Making choices is not always easy, but it is something students will have to do daily for the rest of their lives. Ask students why it is important to take responsibility for their choices.

READ IT *If You Had to Choose, What Would You Do?* (pages 37–39).

DO IT Students complete the "Choice Week" activity sheet. Students record the good and bad choices they make during the week.

TALK ABOUT IT At the end of the week, have students share the choices they made and how they rated each choice. Brainstorm with the group examples of how people can choose good things for themselves and how they can hurt themselves with poor choices. Tell students that the power to choose wisely is one of the most important skills they can learn.

WRITE ABOUT IT In their journals, students respond to the prompt: Describe the connection between accountability and making good choices.

Think Before You Act

LEARNING OBJECTIVE

Students will:

- learn how to manage their emotions before they react to difficult situations

MATERIALS NEEDED

The book *Life Lists for Teens* by Pamela Espeland, "Think Before You Act" activity sheet (page 173), and pencils or pens

LESSON PLAN

CHECK IT Ask students to describe tough situations they have been in where their emotions overcame them. Ask students: How should we respond to these types of situations? When someone puts us down, threatens us, or spreads rumors about us, we might choose to respond quickly without thinking about the consequences of our actions. How can we avoid this?

READ IT *Life Lists for Teens*, "4 Steps to Feeling Peaceful" (page 15).

DO IT Students complete the "Think Before You Act" activity sheet in small groups. Allow time for students to share and compare how they can calm themselves down in order to respond to conflict in a positive way. Have them make a list of solutions.

TALK ABOUT IT Have students share what they learned in their small groups. Ask: Did you learn any new ways to calm yourself? Review the Stop, Think, Choose steps (page 49).

WRITE ABOUT IT In their journals, students respond to the prompt: What works best to calm you down when you get upset?

Making a Difference at Our School

LEARNING OBJECTIVE

Students will:

- learn ways they can help make their school a safe and caring place

MATERIALS NEEDED

The book *Making Every Day Count* by Pamela Espeland and Elizabeth Verdick, "Making a Difference at Our School" activity sheet (page 174), and pencils or pens

LESSON PLAN

CHECK IT Ask students: Do you feel you have had an opportunity to make a positive difference in your school? Everyone should feel free to try to change things for the better.

READ IT *Making Every Day Count*, "April 27" (page 118).

DO IT Students complete the "Making a Difference at Our School" activity sheet. Students record positive ways they can affect their school community.

TALK ABOUT IT Review the completed activity sheets. As a class, make a list of the most creative ways students can help their school become inclusive, bully free, and safe for everyone.

WRITE ABOUT IT In their journals, students respond to the prompt: What does school pride mean to you?

Making Wise Choices

LEARNING OBJECTIVE

Students will:

- review what they have learned this month about making choices

MATERIALS NEEDED

The book *Making Every Day Count* by Pamela Espeland and Elizabeth Verdick, "Making Wise Choices" activity sheet (page 175), and pencils or pens

LESSON PLAN

CHECK IT Review the monthly theme with the class. Have students explain what they have learned this month about choices and decision making.

READ IT *Making Every Day Count*, "July 25" (page 207).

DO IT Students complete the "Making Wise Choices" activity sheet. Students complete a crossword using April's thematic words.

TALK ABOUT IT Review the completed crossword puzzles. *Answers: Across: 2-brave, 3-predict, 6-positive, 8-option, 12-reflect, 13-responsible, 14-decide, 15-consequence. Down: 1-negative, 4-choice, 5-anger, 7-outcome, 9-helpless, 10-mistake, 11-forgive.*

WRITE ABOUT IT In their journals, students respond to the prompt: This month I learned that I am responsible for...

The Power to Choose Quiz

To assess student progress, use the quiz on page 176. *(Answers: 1-T, 2-T, 3-F, 4-T, 5-T, 6-d, 7-a, 8-d, 9-learn, mistakes, 10-choose, difference)*

Safe & Caring Vocabulary

Fill in the blanks below with the correct words from the list:

consequences	common sense	different	know
choices	tough	affect	support
help	impulse	predict	life
determine	trust	stop	consideration
easy	facts	think	problem

_ _ _ _ is full of _ _ _ _ _ _ _. Some choices are _ _ _ _ to make and

just need _ _ _ _ _ _ _ _ _ _ _, but others are _ _ _ _ _ and require you to

_ _ _ _ _ _ _ _ _ the _ _ _ _ _. Choices have _ _ _ _ _ _ _ _ _ _ _ _ that can

_ _ _ _ _ _ you and others around you. It is important to _ _ _ _ _ _ _

what might happen instead of acting on _ _ _ _ _ _ _ without careful

_ _ _ _ _ _ _ _ _ _ _ _ _ _. _ _ _ _ and _ _ _ _ _ about the _ _ _ _ _ _ _, how

you feel about it, and then weigh the _ _ _ _ _ _ _ _ _ choices you have.

If you need _ _ _ _, ask someone you _ _ _ _ and _ _ _ _ _ for _ _ _ _ _ _ _.

Define the word **recommendation**. _____

_____

_____

Write a paragraph using the words **impulse**, **alternative**, and **consequences**. _____

_____

_____

_____

_____

we are
a safe
& caring
school.

SaFE & CaRiNG WORD FIND

Find and circle the words listed at the bottom of the page.

(Hint: Answers can run forward, backward, up, down, or diagonally.)

A	G	R	I	T	R	P	F	O	G	U	R	O
U	A	L	T	E	R	N	A	T	I	V	E	Y
O	C	B	H	D	J	X	C	Y	H	R	F	T
P	C	H	O	I	C	E	E	T	T	O	E	L	I
R	O	U	R	S	O	U	S	S	R	C	E	L
E	U	W	I	N	C	B	L	G	E	X	N	C	B
C	N	E	E	N	H	Q	N	B	E	T	O	I
C	T	I	F	R	E	E	D	O	M	U	O	L	S
O	A	N	T	D	N	B	R	L	H	Q	Q	L	I
M	B	E	E	N	G	A	T	I	V	E	E	N
E	I	G	B	H	C	B	J	G	L	S	R	A	P
N	L	R	U	R	I	X	N	N	A	N	P
D	I	E	C	I	T	S	U	Q	O	N	S	S
A	T	G	N	R	O	H	I	R	C	C	E	E
T	Y	Y	R	E	V	A	R	B	O	R	E	R	A
I	P	R	E	D	I	C	T	I	O	N	J	A
O	E	R	U	S	S	E	R	P	T	R	S	B
N	O	I	T	A	N	I	G	A	M	I	G	O

ACCOUNTABILITY	CHOICE	POWER	PRESSURE
RECOMMENDATION	FACTS	HONESTY	BRAVERY
IMAGINATION	RESPONSIBILITY	INTEGRITY	NEGATIVE
PREDICTION	FREEDOM	DECISIONS	TOLERANCE
CONSEQUENCE	ALTERNATIVE	DISCERN	REFLECT

I HAVE THE POWER TO CHOOSE

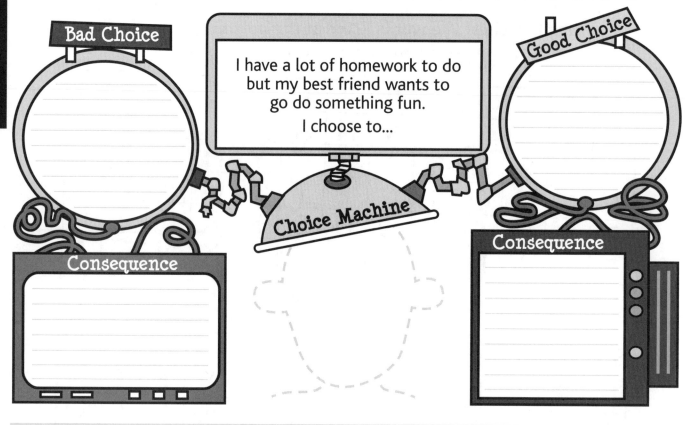

Bad Choice

I have a lot of homework to do but my best friend wants to go do something fun.
I choose to...

Good Choice

Choice Machine

Consequence

Consequence

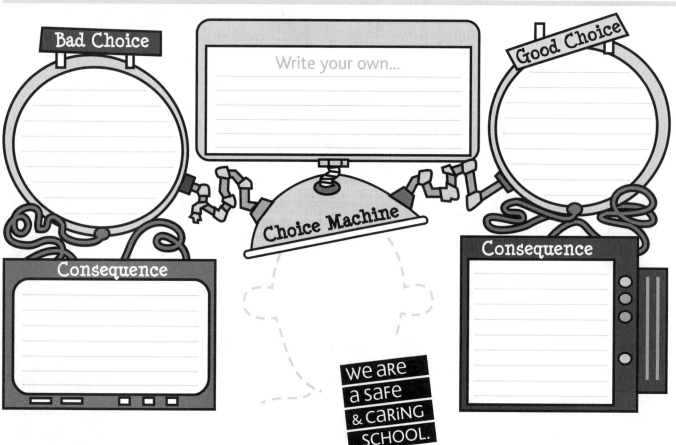

Bad Choice

Write your own...

Good Choice

Choice Machine

Consequence

Consequence

WE ARE
A SAFE
& CARING
SCHOOL.

TARGETING GOOD CHOICES

Sometimes when we feel stressed, we have a hard time making good choices.

Below are choices people make when they feel worried, frustrated, sad, or afraid. Draw a line to target a good choice ⊕ or a bad choice ⊖.

- sleep all day
- listen to music
- talk to someone you trust
- skip school
- draw a picture or cartoon
- eat too much
- read a book
- act out in some way
- take a walk or run
- ignore your homework
- write in a journal
- watch TV all day
- go for a bike ride
- refuse to leave your room
- ask for help

Select one ⊕ choice from above and explain why it's ⊕.

_____

_____

_____

Select one ⊖ choice from above and explain why it's ⊖.

_____

_____

_____

we are a safe & caring school.

WHO IS IN CHARGE OF YOU?

Have you ever done something you didn't want to do just to be part of a group?

Taking responsibility for our actions is very important. Write a story about peer pressure.

By _____

we are
a safe
& caring
school.

MAKING POSITIVE CHOICES

Situation	How would you feel?	What would you choose to do?	What might happen?
Someone is gossiping about you.			
A couple of kids threaten to hurt a classmate if she doesn't share her homework.			
Someone dares you to do something wrong so you can be part of the "cool" group.			
A friend is being bullied by a group of kids.			
Someone laughed at you when you shared your ideas in class.			
You are excluded from an activity.			
Someone makes rude comments about your culture.			

we are a safe & caring school.

WHEEL OF CHOICES

Name-Calling

Gossiping

Threatening

Bullying

Stealing

Blaming

Wheel of Choices

Lying

Negative peer pressure

1) Cut out

2) Glue to card stock

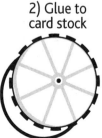

3) Use a fastener to attach wheel to blank sheet

4) Glue the pointer to the sheet

we are a safe & caring school.

LEARNING FROM OUR CHOICES

Describe a poor choice you have made.

> Everybody makes mistakes, but some of us are better than others at learning from them.

What were the consequences of your choice?

What did you learn from making this choice?

we are a safe & caring school.

APRIL

171

From *Safe & Caring Schools® Grades 6–8* by Katia S. Petersen, Ph.D., copyright © 2008. Free Spirit Publishing Inc., Minneapolis, MN; www.freespirit.com. This page may be photocopied for individual, classroom, or small group work only. For other uses, call 800-735-7323.

CHOICE WEEK

Being **accountable** means taking responsibility for your choices. List the important choices you made this week.

Good choices you made   **Bad** choices you made   **How did it feel?**
Circle one of the emotions.

	Good choices you made	Bad choices you made	How did it feel?
Monday			
Tuesday			
Wednesday			
Thursday			
Friday			
Saturday			
Sunday			

Write about a poor choice you made above. How can you be accountable and make things better?

Choice you made	How to be accountable

we are a safe & caring school.

APRIL

THINK BEFORE YOU ACT

Sometimes when we feel upset, angry, or anxious, we say or do things that get us into trouble.

Explain a time when you said or did something before you thought things through.

What did you learn?

How can you calm yourself next time?

What happened?

What were the consequences?
How did your actions affect those around you?

APRIL

we are
a safe
& caring
school.

MAKING A DIFFERENCE AT OUR SCHOOL

How can you and your friends make your school a Safe & Caring place?

Fill in the blanks below with ways you can be helpful in your school and classroom.

Ways we can help

1. We can be an example for others by...

2. We can be positive bystanders by...

3. We can look out for each other by...

4. We can have pride in our school community by...

we are a safe & caring school.

Making Wise Choices

APRIL

Across:
2. Describes someone who makes a hard choice.
3. To guess what will happen.
6. Has good results.
8. A choice.
12. To think about something that has happened.
13. Describes someone who follows through.
14. To make a choice.
15. The result of an action.

Down:
1. Has bad results.
4. An option.
5. What we feel when we get mad.
7. The result of a choice.
9. How a person feels without support.
10. Something everyone makes sometimes.
11. To give someone another chance.

we are
a safe
& caring
school.

THE POWER TO CHOOSE QUIZ

True or False (circle the correct answer)

1) Part of choosing wisely is to consider the consequences of our choices. . . . . **True / False**

2) We can learn from our successes as well as our mistakes. . . . . **True / False**

3) If things don't work out the way you planned, it's best to have someone to blame
so you're not responsible. . . . . **True / False**

4) Learning to be assertive in conflicts takes courage, and sometimes we need to get help. . . . . **True / False**

5) We can make a difference at school and at home when we are accountable for our choices. . . . **True / False**

Multiple Choice (circle the correct answer)

6) At our Safe & Caring School:
   - **a.** others make all the choices for us.
   - **b.** we have the support to consider our options and their consequences.
   - **c.** we learn that we are in charge of ourselves, which means we take responsibility
     for the choices we make.
   - **d.** b and c

7) When we are stressed-out:
   - **a.** we need to think before we act.
   - **b.** it's easiest to quit.
   - **c.** we should ignore our problems, they'll eventually go away.
   - **d.** all of the above

8) Good friends help us:
   - **a.** stay out of trouble.
   - **b.** Stop, Think, Choose before making important decisions.
   - **c.** make connections with the cool kids who do dangerous things.
   - **d.** a and b

Fill in the Blanks

9) Take time to l_____ from your m_____.

10) When you c_____to make a d_____ at your school, everyone wins.

Real-Life Writing

Some kids want to be your friends, but they think you care too much about school and other students.
You'd like to be friends, but you believe in doing your part to make a difference at school.
What do you choose to do?

From *Safe & Caring Schools® Grades 6–8* by Katia S. Petersen, Ph.D., copyright © 2008. Free Spirit Publishing Inc., Minneapolis, MN; www.freespirit.com. This page may be photocopied for individual, classroom, or small group work only. For other uses, call 800-735-7323.

MAY
Follow Your Dreams

- **Goal Setting**
- **Perseverance**
- **Celebration of Self**

Monthly Objectives

Students will:

- understand the importance of facing challenges with persistence and positive attitudes
- realize that having dreams and hopes helps them plan for the future
- learn how to set goals and plan the steps to achieve them
- self-evaluate and celebrate their growth and successes during the year

Social Emotional Definitions

Accomplishment: The successful completion of a task.

Approval: A favorable opinion or feeling about something or someone.

Celebration: A special occasion to acknowledge an accomplishment or something good that happened.

Competitive: Trying to do something better than someone else. Striving to win.

Effort: Giving your best attempt to accomplish something.

Encouragement: Support received from others that inspires confidence and determination to reach a goal.

Flexibility: The ability to change plans, opinions, or direction.

Goal: A task that someone desires to accomplish.

Hero: A person you choose to look up to or want to be like because of his or her abilities and talents.

Inspiration: Something that stimulates your creativity and willingness to accomplish a goal.

Organization: The ability to plan ahead to get things done.

TEACHING TIPS

- Help students connect new learning to real-life experiences.
- Develop the power of young minds by stirring their imagination through creative play, thinking, and writing.
- Improve children's well-being by letting them know you believe in them.
- Recognize small accomplishments on a daily basis. Success brings more success.

MAY INTEGRATED ACTIVITIES

In addition to the specific lesson plans for this month, you can use these optional ideas to integrate and extend the Safe & Caring themes into your daily routines and across curricular areas.

LANGUAGE ARTS

- Have students write a short story about something they wish they could do better.
- Have students write an essay about dreams they have for the future. Collect the essays and read one or two each day without sharing the name of the student authors. Ask the group to guess whose dreams they learned about. This activity helps students realize that everyone has hopes and dreams regardless of their gender, culture, socioeconomic status, abilities, and so on.

LITERATURE

- Have students read books dealing with motivation, self-discipline, and perseverance, such as *Helen Keller* by Margaret Davidson or *Teacher: Anne Sullivan Macy* by Helen Keller.
- As a class, talk about great people in history who succeeded in life because they chose not to give up on their dreams. Encourage students to read books about such people, for example, *Louis Braille: The Boy Who Invented Books for the Blind* by Margaret Davidson and *The Wright Brothers: Pioneers of American Aviation* by Quentin Reynolds.

SOCIAL STUDIES

- Invite special guests (parents, community members, school staff) to share information with students about their careers.
- Organize a "Career Day" and help students present reports on people in different jobs.
- Watch the movie *Homeward Bound*. Ask students to write about two or three examples of perseverance in the movie.

ART

- Create a classroom book called "Following Your Dreams." Students write down and draw pictures showing their dreams and ways they can reach them.
- Students create collages using words and images that represent people's dreams and accomplishments.
- Create posters titled "Our Gifts and Talents." Decorate hallways, the entryway, the cafeteria, or other public areas in your school.

MATH

- Read *Mathematicians Are People, Too: Stories from the Lives of Great Mathematicians* by Luetta Reimer and Wilbert Reimer about inspirational moments of mathematical discovery experienced by Thales, Pythagoras, Hypatia, Galileo, Pascal, Germain, and other mathematicians.
- Create a graph that shows how many students have certain types of talent.
- Compare numbers of male versus female students who aspire to certain careers.

MUSIC

- Read *Moses Goes to a Concert* by Isaac Millman. A group of deaf children is taken to a concert where they meet the percussionist, a friend of their teacher, and learn to their surprise that she is also deaf. Discuss the importance of perseverance.
- Have students research child prodigies who used self-discipline and determination to succeed. Students write a report on a specific artist and listen to their music.

SCIENCE

- Students research and document various science careers. Choose a famous scientist from the past or present, and discuss the impact of this person's scientific contribution to the world.

Safe & Caring Vocabulary and Word Find

LEARNING OBJECTIVES

Students will:

- be introduced to the vocabulary that supports learning how to follow their dreams
- internalize the vocabulary as they use it throughout the month and year in real-life situations

MATERIALS NEEDED

"Safe & Caring Vocabulary" (page 184) and "Safe & Caring Word Find" (page 185) activity sheets, pencils, and dictionaries

LESSON PLAN

Use the vocabulary activities to introduce the concepts and common language associated with this month's theme. Throughout the month, use the words in writing, spelling, storytelling, and dealing with conflict situations.

For "Safe & Caring Vocabulary," explain how to unscramble the words to decipher the message. (As you get older, you may start **_thinking_** about where you are going and what you would like to do with your life. Once you find something to **_focus_** on, **_persevere_** so you give yourself a chance to see where your **_strengths_** and **_talents_** lie. It is normal to change your **_direction_** from time to time as you try various options. **_Exploring_** different **_learning_** experiences and **_career_** possibilities can be a lot of work, so make sure to have fun and keep a sense of **_humor_**. Make friends and find good teachers and supporters. **_Encouragement_** will help you stay **_motivated_**. Remember, dreams are important. When you combine dreams with **_goals_**, you can focus your **_efforts_**. When your goals have a **_purpose_**, a **_schedule_**, and **_action_** steps, you can make your dreams come **_true_**.)

For "Safe & Caring Word Find," discuss what the words mean after completing the page. You may want students to work in pairs to help each other.

For an added challenge, at the end of each month, have students work individually or in small groups to create their own word find puzzles, using the words defined in "Social Emotional Definitions" (see page 177).

My Gifts & Talents

LEARNING OBJECTIVES

Students will:

- explore their unique gift and talents
- learn that they can use and develop their strengths to achieve their goals

MATERIALS NEEDED

The book *You Can Do It!* by Erin Falligant and Michelle Watkins, "My Gifts & Talents" activity sheet (page 186), and pencils or pens

LESSON PLAN

CHECK IT Ask students: What is *talent*? Where do talents come from? Do you have a special talent? Introduce the importance of recognizing and developing one's individual strengths.

READ IT *You Can Do It!* shows girls that whatever they dream, they can do.

DO IT Students complete the "My Gifts & Talents" activity sheet. Students think about what makes them unique.

TALK ABOUT IT Students share information from the activity sheets. Encourage them to take risks and try new things that will help them grow. Students sometimes wish they could have someone else's gifts and don't recognize their own abilities. Encourage them to appreciate their own assets.

WRITE ABOUT IT In their journals, students respond to the prompt:

My greatest talent is...
A talent I wish I had is...

MORE COOL READS *Bud, Not Buddy* by Christopher Paul Curtis is about a 10-year-old boy in Depression-era Michigan, who sets out to find the man he believes to be his father.

I Can Do Anything!

LEARNING OBJECTIVES

Students will:

- learn to identify their goals
- learn how to determine and plan the steps needed to accomplish their goals

MATERIALS NEEDED

The book *Amelia Earhart* by Jane Sutcliffe, "I Can Do Anything!" activity sheet (page 187), dictionaries, and pencils or pens

LESSON PLAN

CHECK IT Ask students to define the word *perseverance*. Relate it to their plans for the future. Have students brainstorm and create a list of specific skills they can use to achieve their goals, such as having a plan, being consistent, learning to be flexible, asking for help and suggestions, being persistent, and having patience.

READ IT Read *Amelia Earhart*. Amelia Earhart made history by being the first woman to fly across the Atlantic Ocean. How did she persevere in her goal?

DO IT Students complete the "I Can Do Anything!" activity sheet. Students write about their dreams and what it will take to reach those dreams.

TALK ABOUT IT Review completed activity sheets with students. Discuss the importance of having a plan. A plan helps students feel more organized and gives them a place to start. Recognize students' work and perseverance as they strive to attain their goals.

WRITE ABOUT IT In their journals, students respond to the prompt: Write about what success means to you and how perseverance can help you reach your goals.

MORE COOL READS *Madam C. J. Walker* by Lori Hobkirk is the biography of Sarah Breedlove Walker who, though born in poverty, was a pioneer in cosmetics for black women and achieved great financial success.

Which Way Will I Go?

LEARNING OBJECTIVES

Students will:

- explore different career possibilities
- learn to stay flexible as they consider their options

MATERIALS NEEDED

The book *145 Things to Be When You Grow Up* by Jodi Weiss and Russell Kahn, "Which Way Will I Go?" activity sheet (page 188), and pencils or pens

LESSON PLAN

CHECK IT Ask students to name careers they are interested in. Ask: How many of you have already changed your minds at least once about careers? Explain that as they grow, students may change their minds because their interests or needs may change.

READ IT *145 Things to Be When You Grow Up* will open students' eyes to a world of career possibilities and give them an idea of what to expect down each career path. Select the careers your students named and read about them aloud.

DO IT Students complete the "Which Way Will I Go?" activity sheet. Allow students time to research and record three career choices.

TALK ABOUT IT Discuss with students their many career opportunities. Explain that when they have a vision, a good support system, and self-confidence, they can succeed in anything they choose.

WRITE ABOUT IT In their journals, students respond to the prompt: A career I always wanted to explore is...

MORE COOL READS *Catherine, Called Birdy* by Karen Cushman is about Birdy, the daughter of an English nobleman in the year 1290, who looks with a clear and critical eye upon the world around her, telling of the people she knows and of the daily events in her small manor house.

Positive Role Models

LEARNING OBJECTIVES

Students will:

- recognize their strengths and talents
- identify their heroes

MATERIALS NEEDED

The book *Christopher Reeve: Actor and Activist* by Margaret L. Finn, the book *Kids with Courage* by Barbara A. Lewis, "Positive Role Models" activity sheet (page 189), and pencils or pens

LESSON PLAN

CHECK IT Ask students to describe what makes someone a role model. Ask them about family, friends, or current or historical figures they admire and wish they could be like.

READ IT *Christopher Reeve: Actor and Activist* (pages 71–85) is the biography of the actor who gained fame playing Superman in the movies and took on a new role as activist after becoming a quadriplegic. Also read *Kids with Courage: True Stories About Young People Making a Difference*.

DO IT Students complete the "Positive Role Models" activity sheet.

TALK ABOUT IT Review completed activity sheets. Discuss people who have had a positive influence on students' lives. Celebrate students' individual gifts and talents.

WRITE ABOUT IT In their journals, students respond to the prompt: Write about a person who has inspired you and why.

MORE COOL READS *Journey to Jamestown* by Lois Ruby. Apprenticed to a barber-surgeon, Elias sets sail for a new life in the Jamestown Colony where he discovers that he has a knack for healing.

Job Pictionary

LEARNING OBJECTIVES

Students will:

- explore the different careers found in their community
- learn about the many career choices they have

MATERIALS NEEDED

The book *If You Could Be Anything, What Would You Be?* by Jeanne Webster, "Job Pictionary" template (page 190), and scissors

LESSON PLAN

CHECK IT Reaching one's dream takes time, planning, and the exploration of how to best use individual gifts and talents. Have students brainstorm what kinds of careers people have around their school, neighborhood, or community. Make a list of the jobs that sound interesting to the students and discuss the skills necessary for each job.

READ IT *If You Could Be Anything, What Would You Be?* (pages 9–15) helps students design their perfect career map and learn how to achieve it.

DO IT Cut out the words on the activity sheet and use them to play "Job Pictionary." Students take turns choosing and drawing one of the careers, while the rest of the class guesses.

TALK ABOUT IT Ask students which careers from Job Pictionary they want to explore further. Encourage them to learn about more careers by visiting workplaces in their community, doing research on the Internet, or talking to family members, friends, and neighbors.

WRITE ABOUT IT In their journals, students respond to the prompt: A career I have always been interested in is…

MORE COOL READS *The Teenagers' Guide to School Outside the Box* by Rebecca Greene encourages readers to think about what they are interested in and choose an opportunity to learn about it outside the classroom.

Go for It!

LEARNING OBJECTIVE

Students will:

- identify a goal and create a three-step plan to attain it

MATERIALS NEEDED

The book *What Do You Really Want?* by Beverly K. Bachel, "Go for It!" activity sheet (page 191), transparency, and pencils or pens

LESSON PLAN

CHECK IT Ask students: Have you ever felt like giving up while working on something you felt was too hard? Discuss how to break down a goal into smaller steps so that students can accomplish it without feeling overwhelmed.

READ IT *What Do You Really Want?*, "The Goal-Getter Action Plan" (pages 48–58) helps readers learn about setting smaller goals to accomplish the large goal.

DO IT Students complete the "Go for It!" activity sheet. Using the transparency, take an ordinary goal, like improving a basketball shot or becoming a better writer, and break it down into smaller, more manageable steps. Explain that when we want to accomplish something, we need to have a plan that includes people who can help us reach our goals. Encourage students to create their own step-by-step plan for success by thinking through immediate and long-term goals.

TALK ABOUT IT Review the activity sheets. Students share some of their dreams and how they plan to reach them. Help them understand that sometimes it may take a long time to reach a goal.

WRITE ABOUT IT In their journals, students respond to the prompt: Write about a time you felt like giving up on a goal. Did anyone help you? What did you learn from the experience?

MORE COOL READS *What Teens Need to Succeed* by Peter Benson, Judy Galbraith, and Pamela Espeland describes 40 Developmental Assets that teenagers need to succeed in life, such as family support and positive peer influences, and suggests ways to acquire these assets.

Stick to It!

LEARNING OBJECTIVES

Students will:

- learn the importance of perseverance in helping them accomplish their goals
- learn that challenges can teach us new ways to reach our goals

MATERIALS NEEDED

The book *What Do You Really Want?* by Beverly K. Bachel, paper, and pencils or pens

LESSON PLAN

CHECK IT Explain that working on one's goals is not always an easy task. Everybody finds challenges along the way as they try to accomplish something. Ask students to imagine the end result and to stick to that vision until they accomplish their goal. Ask: How many of you have experienced challenges as you tried to meet one of your goals? What did you learn from that experience?

READ IT *What Do You Really Want?*, "Goal-Getters in Action" (pages 93–103) explains that sometimes we fail to complete our goals and why.

DO IT Divide the class into small groups. Each group designates a leader and a recorder. Students discuss the difficulties they have in sticking to their goal plan, imagining an end to the process, and grappling with the potential for failure. Ask the group to devise a strategy for staying focused and motivated. Have each group record their ideas and be ready to share.

TALK ABOUT IT Ask students: Where do you get support when the going gets rough? Do you ever feel like giving up? What can you do to get inspired again and move forward? Remind students that people (such as you) believe in them and will give them the support they need to succeed.

WRITE ABOUT IT In their journals, students respond to the prompt: To reach my goal, I need support from...

My Dreams & Wishes

LEARNING OBJECTIVES

Students will:

- learn how to visualize their future
- learn how to develop a plan to help them attain goals for the future

MATERIALS NEEDED

The book *What Do You Really Want?* by Beverly K. Bachel, "My Dreams & Wishes" activity sheet (page 192), transparency, and pencils or pens

LESSON PLAN

CHECK IT Ask students to take a few minutes to think about their vision and dreams for the future. Why is it important to have dreams and plans for the future? What is needed to make those dreams come true? Discuss how dreams need a step-by-step plan to make them become a reality. Discuss action steps and have students create a list of people who can act as their mentors along the way.

READ IT *What Do You Really Want?*, "What Is a Goal?" (pages 1–2) explains how a goal is different from a dream.

DO IT Using the overhead transparency, show students how to develop step-by-step plans that will help them realize their dreams. For example: *My dream* is to become a scientist. *My wish for my dream* is to attend college. *The steps I plan to take* are to continue to study hard, get good grades, ask for help when I need it, research colleges, look for scholarship possibilities, interview scientists, and volunteer during the summer. *I know my plan is working when* I've been accepted at a college with a good science program where I'll have the opportunity to begin realizing my dream.

TALK ABOUT IT Review information from the activity sheets. Remind students that their dreams may change over time, especially as they learn more about themselves or are inspired by others. Some people know early on what they wish to do in life. Others have to try several different paths before they find something that's right for them. Encourage students not to stress about having all the answers about their future or trying to live up to others' expectations of them.

WRITE ABOUT IT In their journals, students respond to the prompt: What's the toughest thing about making my dream a reality?

MORE COOL READS *What Color Is Your Parachute? For Teens* by Richard Nelson Bolles and Carol Christen teaches high school and college students to zero in on their favorite skills and apply that knowledge to get the most out of school, set goals, and find their dream jobs. Also read *Young Person's Occupational Outlook Handbook* by Jist Works.

Self-Discipline

LEARNING OBJECTIVES

Students will:

- learn how self-discipline will help them reach their goals
- create a visual of their dream to help keep them motivated

MATERIALS NEEDED

The book *Wilma Unlimited* by Kathleen Krull, magazines, poster paper, scissors, glue, and photographs of the students (if available)

LESSON PLAN

CHECK IT   Tell students that *self-discipline* is the ability to pursue a goal, especially in the face of conflict. It's also the ability to think through situations, make a plan, and follow through by making the best choices possible.

READ IT   Read *Wilma Unlimited*. Because of her perseverance and determination, Wilma Rudolph became the first woman to win three Olympic gold medals, despite suffering from polio.

DO IT   Divide students into small groups. Each student creates a collage—a collection of pictures, words, drawings, or other materials—showing their dreams and goals.

TALK ABOUT IT   Have the students explain their collages to the class. Ask students: What support and guidance will you need to achieve your goals? Do you believe you have the strength to maintain the self-discipline and determination necessary to complete your goals? Are you ready to work hard to attain your dreams?

WRITE ABOUT IT   In their journals, students respond to the prompt: What have you learned about self-discipline that will help you reach your goals in the future?

MORE COOL READS   *What Do You Really Want?* by Beverly K. Bachel, "Don't Give Up" (pages 88–89).

How I Did This Year

LEARNING OBJECTIVE

Students will:

- review their accomplishments during the school year

MATERIALS NEEDED

The book *What Do You Really Want?* by Beverly K. Bachel, "How I Did This Year" activity sheet (page 193), and pencils or pens

LESSON PLAN

CHECK IT   Ask the students to share some of the things they feel they have accomplished in the past year. Encourage them to celebrate all their hard work and accomplishments. Have students think about their favorite activities during the year, the challenges they faced along the way, the new friendships they built, and the things that most surprised them.

READ IT   *What Do You Really Want?*, "Reward Yourself" (pages 108–112).

DO IT   Students complete the "How I Did This Year" activity sheet.

TALK ABOUT IT   Students may choose to share with the class things they are proud of, things they wish they had done, and where they see themselves in the future. Ask students to create a list of collective accomplishments and to reflect on the goals they set at the beginning of the year. Emphasize the importance of celebrating their accomplishments and efforts. Encourage them to acknowledge the support they received from people around them.

WRITE ABOUT IT   In their journals, students respond to the prompt: Some things I want to celebrate from this year...

Follow Your Dreams Quiz

To assess student progress, use the quiz on page 194. (*Answers: 1-T, 2-T, 3-T, 4-F, 5-T, 6-d, 7-d, 8-d, 9-perfect, help, 10-learn, succeed*)

SaFe & CaRinG VOCaBULaRY

Unscramble the words to complete the sentences.

As you get older, you may start _ _ _ _ _ _ _ _ about where you are
                                    k i n n i h g t

going and what you would like to do with your life. Once you find

something to _ _ _ _ _ on, _ _ _ _ _ _ _ _ _ so you give yourself a
              u c o f s   r e v r e p s e r

chance to see where your _ _ _ _ _ _ _ _ _ and _ _ _ _ _ _ _ lie.
                           g e t t n h s s r   s a n t l e t

It is normal to change your _ _ _ _ _ _ _ _ _ from time to time as
                              o t i r c e n i d

you try various options. _ _ _ _ _ _ _ _ _ _ different _ _ _ _ _ _ _ _
                           l i x e r o p g n   n a g i l e n r

experiences and _ _ _ _ _ _ possibilities can be a lot of work,
                  e a r r c e

so make sure to have fun and keep a sense of _ _ _ _ _. Make friends
                                               m o h u r

and find good teachers and supporters. _ _ _ _ _ _ _ _ _ _ _ _ _ will
                                         n o m r a e e c u g n

help you stay _ _ _ _ _ _ _ _ _. Remember, dreams are important.
               i d t e m v o a t

When you combine dreams with _ _ _ _ _, you can focus your
                               s l o g a

_ _ _ _ _ _ _. When your goals have a _ _ _ _ _ _ _, a _ _ _ _ _ _ _ _,
f e s t r o f   e s p p u r o   l e s h u d e c

and _ _ _ _ _ _ steps, you can make your dreams come _ _ _ _.
     n i t o c a   r e t u

Define the word **inspiration**. _____

_____

Write a sentence using the words **goals**, **determination**,
and **vision**. _____

_____

_____

_____

we aRe
a SaFe
& CaRinG
SCHOOL.

SAFe & CARiNG WORD FIND

Find and circle the words listed at the bottom of the page.

(Hint: Answers can run forward, backward, up, down, or diagonally.)

A	N	O	I	T	C	E	R	I	D	P	L	I
A	I	N	T	E	L	L	I	G	E	N	C	E	A
N	F	O	C	U	S	N	O	I	T	C	A	Y
S	P	U	V	K	M	C	A	R	E	E	R	G
P	C	S	A	X	P	L	L	C	B	A	N	O
I	O	S	B	I	W	Q	S	U	P	V	E	N
R	N	E	A	V	C	M	W	Q	H	E	R	O
A	S	N	M	P	A	J	P	C	Q	M	N	I
T	I	E	B	U	C	U	O	L	S	O	O	T
I	S	R	I	R	Q	W	V	A	Z	T	O	A
O	T	A	O	L	P	B	I	Y	X	I	I	R
N	E	W	L	M	V	S	S	M	J	V	T	B
U	N	A	C	B	U	Y	S	I	Q	I	A	U	E
M	C	Q	P	H	L	H	O	P	E	T	T	L
A	Y	I	T	U	V	P	N	U	B	E	N	E
V	K	N	O	W	L	E	D	G	E	D	I	C
P	E	R	S	E	V	E	R	A	N	C	E	O
U	A	C	H	A	L	L	E	N	G	E	S	I

LEARNER	RISK	MOTIVATED	DIRECTION
CELEBRATION	INTELLIGENCE	ENTHUSIASM	GOALS
KNOWLEDGE	INTUITION	CHALLENGES	VISION
INSPIRATION	HUMOR	PERSEVERANCE	FOCUS
ACTION	CONSISTENCY	CAREER	HERO

we are
a safe
& caring
SCHOOL.

MY GIFTS & TALENTS

Have you ever asked yourself
what your true talents are, or what
makes you unique?

**Fill in the spaces below to discover the strengths
you have that will help you succeed now and in the future.**

My talents and skills:

_____
_____
_____
_____
_____
_____
_____

Things that are easy for me to do:

_____
_____
_____
_____
_____
_____
_____

One way I have used my skills is:

_____
_____
_____
_____
_____

Things I'd like to get better at:

_____
_____
_____
_____

My dreams for the future are...

_____
_____
_____
_____

we aRe
a saFe
& CaRiNG
SCHOOL.

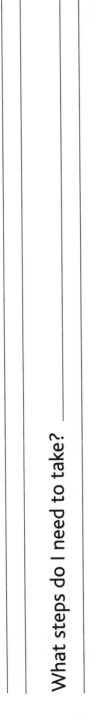

I can do anything!

My Dream: If I can do anything in the world, what will I do? _____

_____

_____

What steps do I need to take? _____

_____

What skills will I need? _____

_____

The hardest part of my dream for me to accomplish might be... _____

_____

I could get some help from... _____

_____

To stay motivated I need to... _____

_____

WE ARE
A SAFE
& CARING
SCHOOL.

WHICH WAY WILL I GO?

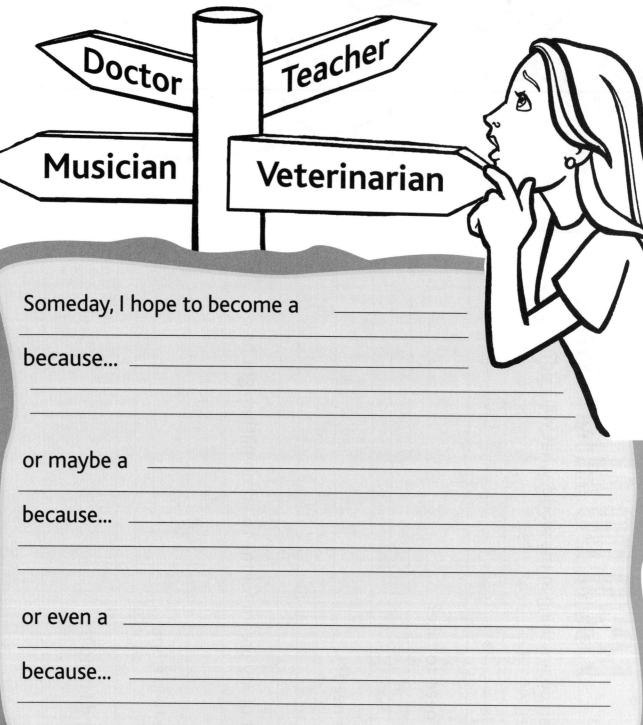

Doctor

Teacher

Musician

Veterinarian

Someday, I hope to become a _____

_____

because... _____

_____

_____

or maybe a _____

_____

because... _____

_____

_____

or even a _____

_____

because... _____

_____

_____

Remember, as you grow, you may discover that your interests change.
It's okay to change your mind about the career path you choose.

we aRe
a SaFe
& CaRiNG
SCHOOL.

POSITIVE ROLE MODELS

...are people with character and skills
we think are really cool.

Who is someone you really look up to and why?

_____
_____
_____

List the qualities you admire in him or her:

• _____   • _____
• _____   • _____
• _____   • _____

What can you do to be more like this person? _____

_____
_____

In the space below, write how you can
make a positive difference in the world.

_____
_____
_____
_____
_____
_____
_____
_____
_____
_____
_____

WE ARE
a SAFE
& CARiNG
SCHOOL.

JOB PICTIONARY

Pilot	Teacher	Athlete
Fire Fighter	Photographer	Doctor
Dentist	Painter	Barber
Ambulance Driver	Musician	Secretary
Train Engineer	Police Officer	Baker
Artist	Judge	Plumber
Music Conductor	Singer	Journalist
Bus Driver	Carpenter	Jockey
Dancer	Scientist	Movie Director
Farmer	Author	TV Announcer
Chef	Lawyer	Engineer

we are
a safe
& caring
school.

GO FOR IT!

My Goal:

Success!

Step 3

Step 2

Step 1

People Who Can Help:

we are a safe & caring school.

My Dreams & Wishes

It's good to have a dream, because then we can think about the steps to make that dream *happen.*

Fill in the blanks below. Take your dream to the next level by thinking through what steps you can take to make it real.

My dream is...

The steps I plan to take...

My wishes for my dream...

I know my plan is working when...

we are a safe & caring school.

HOW I DID THIS YEAR

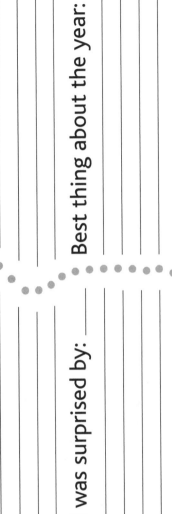

What were your favorite things at school this year?

Write it all here to share with your friends and family!

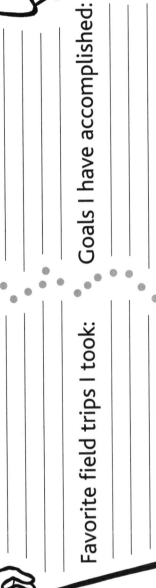

Great people I met: _____

Something new I learned: _____

Goals I have accomplished: _____

Best thing about the year: _____

Best experiences I had: _____

Favorite books I read: _____

Favorite field trips I took: _____

I was surprised by: _____

we are a safe & caring school.

FOLLOW YOUR DREAMS QUIZ

True or False (circle the correct answer)

1) Reading about positive role models inspires us to explore possibilities in life . . . . **True / False**
2) A talent is something that you naturally have. . . . . **True / False**
3) Even if we don't succeed after sticking to a difficult goal, it is still a valuable experience that we can learn from . . . . **True / False**
4) It's better to only do what comes easy; otherwise, it's too much work . . . . **True / False**
5) When we keep trying new things, we build our self-confidence to reach and grow further . . . . . . **True / False**

Multiple Choice (circle the correct answer)

6) At our Safe & Caring School:
   a. we are encouraged to make and achieve goals.
   b. we need to respect each other's dreams.
   c. my support system is there when I need help.
   d. all of the above

7) Thinking about job possibilities:
   a. is useless because I have no idea what I want to do.
   b. gives me a chance to explore where I'm going.
   c. helps me make decisions about what I want to focus on at school.
   d. b and c

8) I can help make the world a Safe & Caring place:
   a. by using Stop, Think, Choose even when I'm not at school.
   b. when I refuse to be pressured by others to do things that make me uncomfortable.
   c. by helping others get along.
   d. all of the above

Fill in the Blanks

9) Role models aren't p_____, they need h_____ sometimes, too.

10) If we persevere and l_____ from our challenges, we will build the skills to s_____.

Real-Life Writing

You are working on a big project that you really want to finish, but there is a lot of work to do, and you want to go have fun with your friends. Everyone needs a break sometimes.
Can you find a balance between your project and play? How?

we are
a safe
& caring
SCHOOL.

RECOMMENDED RESOURCES

BOOKS

All Kids Are Our Kids: What Communities Must Do to Raise Caring and Responsible Children and Adolescents by Peter L. Benson (San Francisco: Jossey-Bass, 1997). Challenges all community members to take responsibility for the development and well-being of the community's children. Emphasizes asset building.

Building Academic Success on Social and Emotional Learning: What Does the Research Say? edited by Joseph E. Zins, Roger P. Weissberg, Margaret C. Wang, and Herbert J. Walberg (New York: Teachers College Press, 2004). Explains the science and research supporting the integration of social and emotional learning (SEL) into school curriculum.

The Bully Free Classroom by Allan L. Beane (Minneapolis: Free Spirit Publishing, 2004). More than 100 bullying prevention and intervention strategies for teachers of grades K–8.

Caring Classrooms/Intelligent Schools: The Social Emotional Education of Young Children edited by Jonathan Cohen (New York: Teachers College Press, 2001). Experts provide tips and strategies for integrating SEL into the school day.

Educating Minds and Hearts: Social Emotional Learning and the Passage into Adolescence edited by Jonathan Cohen (New York: Teachers College Press, 1999). Explains the theory and science supporting SEL and provides overviews of successful SEL programs across the nation.

Emotional Intelligence: Why It Can Matter More than I.Q. by Daniel P. Goleman (New York: Bantam Books, 2006). Explains how and why emotional intelligence is a key factor in determining career success, relationship satisfaction, overall well-being, and more.

Emotionally Intelligent Parenting: How to Raise a Self-Disciplined, Responsible, Socially Skilled Child by Maurice J. Elias, Steve E. Tobias, and Brian S. Friedlander (New York: Harmony Books, 1997). Contains advice and practical strategies on how to foster emotional intelligence in children.

Growing Good Kids: 28 Activities to Enhance Self-Awareness, Compassion, and Leadership by Deb Delisle and Jim Delisle (Minneapolis: Free Spirit Publishing, 1996). Classroom-tested activities for grades 3–8 that build students' skills in problem solving, decision making, cooperative learning, and more.

Higher Expectations: Promoting Social Emotional Learning and Academic Achievement in Your School by Raymond J. Pasi (New York: Teachers College Press, 2001). Helpful advice on how to design and implement a successful SEL program in your classroom, school, and school district.

Multiple Intelligences: The Theory in Practice by Howard Gardner (New York: Basic Books, 1993). Practical applications of multiple intelligence theory for educators.

Promoting Social and Emotional Learning: Guidelines for Educators by Maurice J. Elias (Alexandria, VA: Association for Supervision and Curriculum Development, 1997). Advice on how to advocate for, develop, implement, and evaluate school-wide SEL programs.

Raising a Thinking Child: Help Your Child to Resolve Everyday Conflicts and Get Along with Others by Myrna B. Shure with Theresa Foy DiGeronimo (New York: Henry Holt, 1994). Tips for helping kids become independent thinkers with the self-esteem, self-confidence, and problem-solving skills to handle challenges throughout life.

Resiliency: What We Have Learned by Bonnie Benard (San Francisco: WestEd, 2004). Summarizes ten years of research on resiliency development in children and offers suggestions on how to incorporate and apply the research in everyday life.

What Kids Need to Succeed: Proven, Practical Ways to Raise Good Kids by Peter L. Benson, Judy Galbraith, and Pamela Espeland (Minneapolis: Free Spirit Publishing, 1994). Over 900 suggestions to help adults build Developmental Assets in children at home, at school, and in the community.

ADDITIONAL BOOKS FOR STUDENTS

The Skin I'm In by Sharon G. Flake (New York: Jump at the Sun/Hyperion Books for Children, 2007 reissue). Middle school student Maleeka Madison's dark skin and unstylish clothes draw much teasing and torment. Her English teacher tries to teach her about the power of writing and social standing.

The Misfits by James Howe (New York: Atheneum Books for Young Readers, 2001). A group of seventh-graders who have long been the target of cruel name-calling decide they're not going to take it any more. This is an upbeat novel that encourages preteens and teens to celebrate their individuality.

The Girls by Amy Goldman Koss (New York: Dial Books for Young Readers, 2000). When members of Maya's clique decide to ostracize her, she is shocked and devastated. She has no clue what she could have done wrong. A great story about social status and peer pressure among middle school students.

The Losers' Club by John LeKich (Toronto, Ontario: Annick Press, 2002). A group of kids are bullied and labeled as losers because of their disabilities. Thanks to Alex, a student with cerebral palsy, the group learns about belonging, acceptance, and support and is able to stand up to the bullies.

Stargirl by Jerry Spinelli (New York: Knopf, 2000). A charming and sensitive novel written in diary format about a nonconformist heroine who learns about loss, growing pains, and staying true to herself.

The Revealers by Doug Wilhelm (New York: Farrar, Straus and Giroux, 2003). "The Revealer" is an email forum in which students can relate their backgrounds, interests, and experiences of being bullied. The "silent majority" is riveted and repelled, and suddenly the school's culture takes a turn for the better.

Read All About It! Great Read-Aloud Stories, Poems, and Newspaper Pieces for Preteens and Teens by Jim Trelease (New York: Penguin Books, 1993). Presents a collection of fictional stories, autobiographical pieces, and newspaper columns, arranged for reading aloud.

ORGANIZATIONS/WEB SITES

The Center for Social Emotional Education (CSEE)
1841 Broadway, Suite 1212
New York, NY 10023
800-998-4701
www.csee.net
The CSEE is an organization that helps schools integrate crucial social and emotional learning with academic instruction.

Character Education Partnership (CEP)
1025 Connecticut Avenue NW, Suite 1011
Washington, DC 20036
800-988-8081
www.character.com
A nonprofit organization dedicated to promoting character education at all grade levels. The Web site contains downloadable publications, lesson plans, a character education blog, and a substantive list of resources.

Collaborative for Academic, Social, and Emotional Learning (CASEL)
University of Illinois at Chicago
Department of Psychology
1007 W. Harrison Street
Chicago, IL 60607
312-413-1008
www.casel.org
An organization dedicated to promoting and advancing the practice of SEL. The Web site offers information and resources on all aspects of SEL advocacy and implementation.

Educators for Social Responsibility
23 Garden Street
Cambridge, MA 02138
800-370-2515
www.esrnational.org
A national nonprofit organization that works with educators to advocate practices such as SEL, character development, conflict resolution, diversity education, civic engagement, and more. The Web site contains lesson plans, activities, articles, and links for teachers of all grades.

GoodCharacter.com
www.goodcharacter.com
Recommended by the Parents' Choice Foundation, this Web site contains resources for character development and service learning. Includes articles, tips, teaching guides, lesson plans, and resource lists.

Learning Peace
www.learningpeace.com
This site helps educators, parents, and other adults create more peace in schools, homes, and communities by teaching children conflict resolution, anger management, anti-bullying, and character building.

Search Institute
The Banks Building
615 First Avenue NE, Suite 125
Minneapolis, MN 55413
800-888-7828
www.search-institute.org
Through dynamic research and analysis, this independent nonprofit organization works to promote healthy, active, and content youth and communities through asset building.

Teaching Tolerance
The Southern Poverty Law Center
400 Washington Avenue
Montgomery, AL 36104
334-956-8200
www.tolerance.org
A national education project dedicated to helping teachers foster respect and understanding in the classroom. The Web site contains resources for educators, parents, teens, and kids.

WestEd
730 Harrison Street
San Francisco, CA 94107
877-493-7833
www.wested.org
A nonprofit research, development, and service agency, WestEd enhances and increases education and human development within schools, families, and communities.

ABOUT THE AUTHOR

Katia S. Petersen, Ph.D., is an author, consultant, and educator. She is a training expert in school climate improvement, student support, teacher coaching, and parent engagement. She has delivered professional development courses in schools nationwide on how to use literature to infuse social and emotional learning into core academics. Katia has trained over 65,000 educators and parents to enhance school success.

Katia has received many accolades and awards for her work with children and schools. They include having her books named in the "Top Ten Books" by the National Association of Elementary School Principals; being honored with a Teacher's Choice: Excellence in the Classroom Award from *Teacher Magazine*; and winning the National Association of Broadcasters Service to Children's Television Award.

Katia is the creator of the Safe & Caring Schools program for grades preK–8. She is the president and founder of Petersen Argo, Inc., a consulting firm that has been serving the educational needs of children and adults since 1990. She lives with her family in San Francisco, California.

For more information about Katia, the Safe & Caring Schools program, and training opportunities (on-site workshops, teacher coaching, leadership overview, and more), check out www.safeandcaringschools.com.

SAFE & CARING SCHOOLS PROFESSIONAL DEVELOPMENT

Staff Development and Consultation is available with author Dr. Katia Petersen.

SCS workshops give schools and districts the tools, focus, and planning they need to implement an effective social and emotional learning approach. The options include the following:

- **LEADERSHIP OVERVIEW WORKSHOP**

  For administrators and district leaders who are interested in the benefits of integrating social, emotional, and academic learning and how the SCS program can help accomplish their school improvement goals.

- **SCS ON-SITE WORKSHOP**

  Implement a comprehensive social, emotional, and academic learning approach using the SCS program.

- **TEACHER COACHING**

  Reduce stress and increase creativity among teachers. Hold a staff renewal workshop to bring the warmth back into teamwork and productivity back into the classroom.

- **TRAIN THE TRAINERS WORKSHOP**

  Includes these topics:
  - Teaching the SCS program effectively
  - Philosophy and mission of Safe & Caring Schools
  - Infusing social and emotional learning into academic subject areas
  - Schoolwide and district-wide implementation steps
  - Program sustainability

- **PARENT ENGAGEMENT**

  Reinforce a positive relationship between home and school by introducing parents and caregivers to the SCS approach. Help families practice and reinforce SCS skills at home.

For more information, visit www.safeandcaringschools.com or send an email to info@safeandcaringschools.com.

The Safe & Caring Schools® Series

by Katia S. Petersen, Ph.D.

FLEXIBLE RESOURCE GUIDES THAT BLEND LEARNING WITH LIFE SKILLS AND CHARACTER DEVELOPMENT

Practical activities, monthly themes, and a foundation of literature make it easy to integrate social and emotional learning into the school day. Teacher-created and kid-tested, each resource guide contains complete lesson plans, fun activities, a monthly list of themes with literature connections, reproducible activity sheets, tips for organizing a schoolwide program, and a CD-ROM of all the reproducible activity sheets.

EACH BOOK: *$39.95, Softcover, 208 pp., 8½" x 11", reproducibles, with CD-ROM (Macintosh and Windows compatible)*

Safe & Caring Schools
PreK–K
BOOK WITH CD-ROM

Safe & Caring Schools
Grades 1–2
BOOK WITH CD-ROM

Safe & Caring Schools
Grades 3–5
BOOK WITH CD-ROM

Safe & Caring Schools
Grades 6–8
BOOK WITH CD-ROM

Key features of the Safe & Caring Schools Resources:

MONTHLY THEMES COORDINATED ACROSS ALL GRADE LEVELS

- My Safe & Caring School and Me
- Discovering Our Feelings
- My Support System
- Respect Yourself and Others
- Bullying Prevention
- Teaming Up for Success
- Conflict Resolution
- The Power to Choose
- Follow Your Dreams

SKILLS FOR SCHOOL. SKILLS FOR LIFE.

- Positive behaviors and attitudes
- Prevention of problem behaviors
- Empowering children to be part of the solution
- Getting along with others and celebrating diversity
- Believing in yourself
- Respect and care for others
- Positive adult role models for children
- Thriving as individuals and as part of groups

RESEARCH FOUNDATION

- Tested in various school models and with students of all abilities and backgrounds
- Scientifically-based research shows that social and emotional learning significantly improves students' academic performance
- Teaching approach that educates the whole child
- Integrates social and emotional learning into academic lessons

IMPLEMENTATION PLAN

- Works in all schools
- Use schoolwide or in single classrooms
- Sequential, yet flexible, activities
- Literature-based
- Year-long options
- Activities integrated with core curriculum
- Reproducible activity sheets, also on CD-ROM
- Safe & Caring vocabulary
- Use in morning meetings, advisory time, and throughout the day
- Staff training available

The Safe & Caring Schools® Posters

Ten posters reinforce the lessons and key skills from the Safe & Caring Schools resource guides. Use in classrooms, hallways, and gathering areas throughout the school. All posters are laminated and can be purchased individually or as a set.

EACH POSTER: *$8.95, Laminated, 18" x 24"*
SET OF 10 POSTERS: *$79.95*

POSTERS INCLUDE:
- Ambassadors of Peace
- Break the Silence
- Cool Enough to Care
- Golden Rule
- Be a Good Listener
- Safe & Caring Rules
- Stand Up for What You Believe In
- Stop, Think, Choose
- We Are a Safe & Caring School
- When I Get Angry

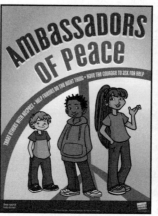
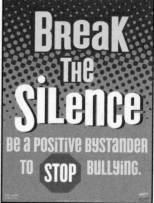

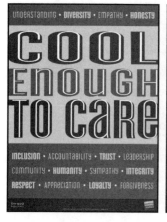

To place an order or to request a free catalog of Self-Help for Kids® and Self-Help for Teens® materials, please write, call, email, or visit our Web site:

Free Spirit Publishing Inc.
217 Fifth Avenue North • Suite 200 • Minneapolis, MN 55401-1299
toll-free 800.735.7323 • local 612.338.2068 • fax 612.337.5050
help4kids@freespirit.com • www.freespirit.com

More great books from Free Spirit

The Complete Guide to Service Learning
Proven, Practical Ways to Engage Students in Civic Responsibility, Academic Curriculum, & Social Action
by Cathryn Berger Kaye, M.A.

A treasury of activities, ideas, quotes, reflections, resources, hundreds of annotated "Bookshelf" recommendations, and author interviews, presented within a curricular context and organized by theme. Grades K–12. *$29.95; 240 pp.; softcover; illust.; 8½" x 11"*

Growing Good Kids
28 Activities to Enhance Self-Awareness, Compassion, and Leadership
by Deb Delisle and Jim Delisle, Ph.D.

Created by teachers and classroom-tested, these fun and meaningful enrichment activities build children's skills in problem solving, decision making, cooperative learning, divergent thinking, and communication. Grades 3–8. *$29.95; 168 pp.; softcover; illust.; 8½" x 11"*

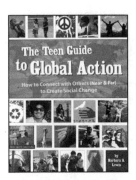

The Teen Guide to Global Action
How to Connect with Others (Near & Far) to Create Social Change
by Barbara A. Lewis

Kids everywhere are acting now to fight hunger and poverty, promote health and human rights, save the environment, and work for peace. They're proving that young people can make a difference locally—and globally. This book includes true stories to inspire young readers, hands-on ideas to get kids excited and involved, fast facts, user-friendly tools, and up-to-date resources kids can use to put their own volunteer spirit into practice. Ages 12 & up. *$12.95; 144 pp.; 2-color; softcover; illust.; 7" x 9"*

Bully Free® Bulletin Boards, Posters, and Banners
Creative Displays for a Safe and Caring School, Grades K–8
by Allan L. Beane, Ph.D., and Linda Beane

Support and reinforce an anti-bullying program or spread the word that bullying won't be tolerated. This book describes 50 displays that kids can create for classrooms, hallways, and other school areas, with instruction and reinforcement from teachers. Each project includes instructions, art templates, visuals, and discussion questions. Grades K–8. *$24.95; 144 pp.; softcover; illust.; 8½" x 11"; lay-flat binding*

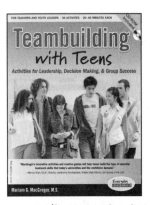

Teambuilding with Teens
Activities for Leadership, Decision Making, & Group Success
by Mariam G. MacGregor, M.S.

Leadership isn't just for a chosen few. All teens can practice the skills and attitudes leaders use. The 36 hands-on activities in this book make learning about leadership meaningful and fun while building character. Kids are called on to recognize each other's strengths, become better listeners, communicate clearly, identify their values, build trust, set goals, and more. The included CD-ROM (for Macintosh and Windows) features all of the reproducible forms from the book. Grades 6–12. *$34.95; 192 pp.; softcover; 8½" x 11"*

The Bully Free Classroom™
Over 100 Tips and Strategies for Teachers K–8
by Allan L. Beane, Ph.D.

Bullying is a big problem in schools today. Allan Beane spells out more than 100 prevention and intervention strategies you can start using immediately. All are easy to understand and simple to implement; many require little or no advance preparation and few or no special materials. Includes 34 pages of reproducible handout masters. Grades K–8. *$24.95; 176 pp.; softcover; 8½" x 11"; lay-flat binding*

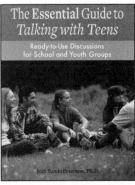

The Essential Guide to Talking with Teens
Ready-to-Use Discussions for School and Youth Groups
by Jean Sunde Peterson, Ph.D.

Tested with thousands of teens in many kinds of schools (plus community centers, churches, and workshops), these guided discussions are proven ways to reach out to young people and address their social and emotional needs. For advising teachers, counselors, and youth workers in all kinds of school and group settings. Grades 6–12. *$29.95; 288 pp.; softcover; 8½" x 11"; lay-flat binding*

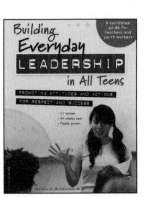

Building Everyday Leadership in All Teens
Promoting Attitudes and Actions for Respect and Success
by Mariam G. MacGregor, M.S., foreword by Barry Z. Posner, Ph.D., Dean and Professor of Leadership at Santa Clara University, California

The sessions in this book guide teens to explore what it means to be a leader, how to work with others, ethical decision-making, risk-taking, team-building, communication, creative thinking, and more. Requires use of the student book, *Everyday Leadership.* Includes reproducibles. Grades 6–12. *$29.95; 208 pp.; softcover; 8½" x 11"*

Mad

How to Deal with Your Anger and Get Respect
by James J. Crist, Ph.D.

Anger is a normal human emotion. But some teens have trouble controlling their anger and get into trouble with their parents, their school, or the law. Practical tools and strategies help them understand and handle their anger and avoid poor decisions and rash actions. Insights from real teens let them know they're not alone. The final chapters explore mental health problems that can complicate anger management and consider the role of counseling and psychotherapy. Includes resources. Ages 13 & up. *$13.95; 160 pp.; 2-color; illust.; softcover; 6" x 9"*

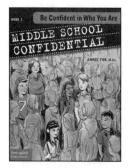

Be Confident in Who You Are

Book 1, Middle School Confidential™ Series
by Annie Fox, M.Ed.

The first book in a series for tweens about the tumultuous middle school years, it offers insider information on common middle school concerns and practical advice for being healthy, feeling good about who you are, and staying in control of your feelings and actions—even when the pressure is on. Filled with character narratives, quizzes, quotes from real kids, tips, tools, and resources, this book is a timely and engaging survival guide for the middle school years. Ages 11–14. *$9.95; 96 pp.; color illust.; softcover; 6" x 8"*

Too Old for This, Too Young for That!

Your Survival Guide for the Middle-School Years
by Harriet S. Mosatche, Ph.D., and Karen Unger, M.A.

Comprehensive, interactive, friendly, and fun, this book helps tweens survive and thrive during middle school. Tips cover everything kids this age care about—physical and emotional changes, family, friends, and school; making decisions; handling peer pressure; setting and reaching goals; and preparing for the years ahead. Ages 10–14. *$14.95; 200 pp.; illust.; softcover; 7" x 9"*

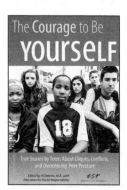

The Courage to Be Yourself

True Stories by Teens About Cliques, Conflicts, and Overcoming Peer Pressure
edited by Al Desetta, M.A., with Educators for Social Responsibility

Cassandra is hassled by her friends for sitting with the "wrong" kids at lunch. Dwan's own family taunts her for not being "black enough." Yen is teased for being Chinese; Jamel for not smoking marijuana. Yet all find the strength to face their conflicts and the courage to be themselves. In 26 first-person stories, real teens write about their lives with searing honesty. They will inspire young readers to reflect on their own lives, work through their problems, and learn who they really are. Ages 13 & up. *$13.95; 160 pp.; softcover; 6" x 9"*

Fighting Invisible Tigers

Stress Management for Teens
(Revised & Updated Third Edition)
by Earl Hipp

Stress is something we all experience. But research suggests that adolescents are affected by it in unique ways that can increase impulsivity and risky behaviors. This book offers proven techniques that teens can use to deal with stressful situations in school, at home, and among friends. They'll find current information on how stress affects health and decision making and learn skills to handle stress in positive ways—including assertiveness, positive self-talk, time management, relaxation exercises, and much more. Filled with interesting facts, student quotes, and fun activities, this book is a great resource for any teen who's said, "I'm stressed out!" Ages 11 & up. *$14.95; 144 pp.; 2-color; illust.; softcover; 6" x 9"*

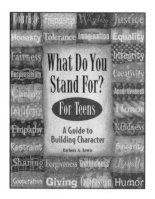

What Do You Stand For? For Teens

A Guide to Building Character
by Barbara A. Lewis

Young people need guidance from caring adults to build strong, positive character traits—but they can also build their own. Quotations and background information set the stage. Dilemmas challenge readers to think about, discuss, and debate positive traits. Activities invite them to explore what they stand for at school, at home, and in their communities. True stories profile real kids who exemplify positive traits; resources point the way toward character-building books, organizations, programs, and Web sites. Ages 11 & up. *$21.95; 288 pp.; B&W photos & illust.; softcover; 8½" x 11"*

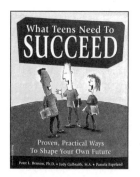

What Teens Need to Succeed

Proven, Practical Ways to Shape Your Own Future
by Peter L. Benson, Ph.D., Judy Galbraith, M.A., and Pamela Espeland

Based on a nationwide survey, this book describes 40 Developmental Assets all teens need to succeed in life, then gives over 1,200 ideas for building assets at home, at school, in the community, in the faith community, and with friends. Includes inspiring true stories, facts, checklists, quizzes, and more. Ages 11 & up. *$15.95; 368 pp.; illust.; softcover; 7¼" x 9¼"*

Bullies Are a Pain in the Brain

written and illustrated by Trevor Romain

Practical suggestions and humor help kids become "Bully-Proof," stop bullies from hurting others, and know what to do in dangerous situations. For ages 8–13. *$8.95; 112 pp.; softcover, illust.; 5⅛" x 7"*

www.freespirit.com